James Gray Stevens

General Rules of the Supreme Court of the Province of New Brunswick

James Gray Stevens

General Rules of the Supreme Court of the Province of New Brunswick

ISBN/EAN: 9783741194306

Manufactured in Europe, USA, Canada, Australia, Japa

Cover: Foto ©Lupo / pixelio.de

Manufactured and distributed by brebook publishing software
(www.brebook.com)

James Gray Stevens

General Rules of the Supreme Court of the Province of New Brunswick

OF

THE SUPREME COURT

OF THE

PROVINCE OF NEW BRUNSWICK

FROM EASTER TERM, 25 GEORGE III, (1875), TO HILARY
TERM, 43 VICTORIA, (1880).

AND OF

THE ELECTION COURT

UNDER THE

DOMINION CONTROVERTED ELECTIONS ACT OF 1874.

———

COLLECTED AND ALPHABETICALLY ARRANGED WITH INDEX OF CONTENTS,

BY

JAMES GRAY STEVENS, Q.C.,

*Judge of County Courts of the Counties of Charlotte, Carleton, Victoria
and Madawaska.*

———
\

CARSWELL & CO.,

TORONTO, ONTARIO, AND EDINBURGH, SCOTLAND.

1880.

CONTENTS.

CONTENTS.

GENERAL ·RULES

OF

THE SUPREME COURT,

OF THE

PROVINCE OF NEW BRUNSWICK.

FROM EASTER TERM 25 GEO. III. 1785, TO HILARY TERM,
43 VICTORIA, 1880.

COLLATED AND ALPHABETICALLY ARRANGED.

ABATEMENT (PLEAS IN.)
Michaelmas Term, 7 Victoria, 1843.

1—*Ordered.* That no plea in abatement shall be filed after the expiration of the rule to plead.

AFFIDAVITS.
Hilary Term, 11 Victoria, 1848.

2—1st. **Illiterate Persons.**

It is ordered, That from and after the first day of Easter Term next, where any affidavit is taken by any Commissioner of this Court, made by any person unable to write or appearing to be illiterate, the Commissioner taking such affidavit shall himself read over, and, if necessary, explain the affidavit to the party making the same; and shall certify or state in the jurat, that the affidavit was read by him to the deponent, who seemed perfectly to understand the same, and also that the said deponent wrote his or her signature, or made his or her mark, in the presence of the Commissioner taking the said affidavit.

2nd. **Where more than one deponent.**

It is further ordered, That after the time aforesaid, where there are two or more deponents in the same affidavit, the names of the deponents who are sworn thereto shall be specified in the jurat.

Michaelmas Term, 11 Victoria, 1847.

3—**Papers annexed to affidavits.**

It is ordered, That from and after the last day of Hilary Term next, the Judge, Commissioner, or Officer taking any affidavit to which any other paper or papers may be annexed, do at the time of taking such affidavit, mark every such annexed paper with his name, or the initial letters of his name.

1

Easter Term, 11 Victoria, 1848.

4—*It is further ordered,* That the General Rule of Michaelmas Term last, in regard to marking papers annexed to any affidavit, shall not extend to affidavits of service of writs returned by the Sheriff, or other officer, to whom the writs are respectively directed.

Hilary Term, 23 Victoria, 1860.

5—Serving affidavits in equity suits.

It is ordered, That it shall not be necessary in any case where a defendant has not appeared, except in applications on notice for an injunction, to serve a copy of any affidavit to be used on any motion, or the hearing of any petition on such defendant, unless service shall be specially directed by any Judge; and it shall in no case be necessary to serve the opposite party with a copy of any affidavit or service of process, or of service of any notice, or other paper, unless specially ordered.

See further, No. 157, 5.

AGENTS.

Michaelmas Term, 31 George III, 1791.

6—*Ordered by the Court,* That all attorneys practising in this Court, who are non-residents of Fredricton, or the City of Saint John, do appoint an agent at one or other of the said places, and give notice to the Clerk or his Deputy of the name of such Agent, and at which of said places he resides; which notice shall be put up in the Clerk's Office; and that all notices, served on such Agents, respectively, shall be deemed as proper and legal a service as if served upon such attorney.

Hilary Term, 7 William IV, 1837.

7—*Whereas,* It is deemed improper that any clerk in the Office of the Clerk of the Pleas of this Court should act as an agent of any Attorney with or without any remuneration or gratuity, *It is ordered,* That henceforth no Attorney of this Court do employ any such clerk as his agent in any suit or matter pending in this Court, or in the transaction of any business in the office either of the Clerk of the Crown, or Clerk of the Pleas; and that the Clerk of the Pleas do not allow or suffer any clerk or other person employed in his office to act as such agent under any pretence whatsoever.

Trinity Term, 3 Victoria, 1840.

8—1st. *It is further Ordered,* That henceforth no Attorney of this Court do employ any student in the office of a Barrister of this Court, as his Agent in any suit or matter pending in this Court, or in the transaction of any business before a Judge, or in the Office either of the Clerk of the Crown or the Clerk of the Pleas; and that no Barrister of this

Court do suffer any one of his students to act as the Agent of any other Attorney. Provided that this rule shall not extend to prevent the employment by a Barrister, who may himself be the Agent of any Attorney, of any student in his office in the professional business of such Attorney.

2nd. The Judges will in future expect, that in the assessment of damages in vacation, as well as in other matters brought before them out of Court, where the parties do not appear in person, they be attended by a Barrister or Attorney of the Court ; or, where this cannot conveniently be done, that the clerk or student employed to attend on behalf of any Attorney, be of competent experience, skill and knowledge of the business entrusted to him.

APPEAL PAPER.

Hilary Term, 32 Victoria, 1869.

9—It is ordered that hereafter there shall be but one appeal paper and that the Clerk of the Pleas shall enter causes thereon in the following order :

1st. Appeals from the decision of a Judge in Equity.

2nd. Appeals from the Court of Divorce and matrimonial causes.

3rd. Appeals from Court of Probate.

4th. Appeals under the Act 27 Vic., c. 44, for winding-up the affairs of incorporated companies.

5th. Appeals from the County Courts—and, in case of any other appeals not hereinafter provided for, they shall be entered after the County Court Appeals in the order of time in which they may be allowed by law.

All appeals shall be heard in their order, and at the time prescribed by the rules of Court.

COUNTY COURT APPEALS.

Michaelmas Term, 40 Victoria, 1876.

10—1st. *It is Ordered,* That the Appellant from a decision of a Judge of a County Court shall enter the cause on the Appeal Paper, of the term immediately succeeding the receipt by the Clerk of the Pleas, of the proceedings from the Judge; and when such proceedings are received during the term, the cause shall be entered on the Appeal Paper of the Term, subject to the order of the Court as to the time when the same shall be heard.

2nd. In case the appellant shall neglect to enter the appeal on the paper according to Rule 1, or having entered it shall not proceed to argue and support the same, when reached in due course upon the paper during the term, if the appellant shall not proceed to support the appeal pursuant to any Order of the Court made in respect thereof, then and in either of such cases, the respondent may, upon the next or any subsequent common motion day after any such default, move that such appeal be dismissed with costs.

3rd. Causes shall be entered on the Appeal Paper as A. B. Appellant *vs.* C. D. Respondent, and any affidavit used in such cases may be entitled in the same way.

Trinity Term, 31 Victoria, 1868.

11—1st. When the minutes of any decree shall not be settled under the Act 17 Vic., c. 18, s. 32, more than fourteen days before the first of any term, a party intending to appeal therefrom shall enter the cause on the Equity Appeal Paper of the term next after the settling of such minutes, but may obtain the order of a Judge to postpone the hearing of such appeal until the second term thereafter, which order shall be made unless good cause be shewn to the contrary, and such order shall direct the time of serving the grounds of appeal on the opposite party.

2nd. Where an appeal is intended to be made from any order of a Judge in Equity in a cause where no decree is made, and such order shall have been made within fourteen days before the first day of any term, a like order may be made as is provided for in the preceding rule.

3rd. Whenever an appeal is made from a decree or order of the Court or of a Judge in Equity, or from the Court of Divorce and matrimonial causes, or from a Probate Court, the Court may order the whole or any part of the pleadings, evidence, judgment or other proceedings to be printed, and such number of printed copies thereof to be furnished for the use of the Appellate Court as may be deemed necessary, and may make order for the payment of the expenses thereof in the costs of the suit.

4th. **Hearing causes.**

All causes intended for hearing at the Sittings in Equity shall be set down with the Clerk in Equity six days before the first day of the sitting of the Court, and shall be entered by him on a docket to be kept for that purpose; and no cause, not so entered, shall be heard without the order of the Judge sitting in such Court.

APPEARANCE.

Easter Term, 25 George III, 1785.

12—*Ordered*, That where an attorney appears for the defendant, a copy of the declaration, with notice of the rule to plead, shall be served on him, he paying for such copy at the rate of sixpence per sheet, and on default of pleading in twenty days, judgment to be entered, and a writ of inquiry may be executed as aforesaid, a plea being first demanded after the said twenty days.

ASSESSMENT OF DAMAGES.

Trinity Term, 26 George III, 1786.

13—*Ordered*, That in causes where interlocutory judgments have been signed, and the causes of action appear to be upon complicated accounts, the same shall be referred to a jury of inquiry, and judgment shall be considered to be entered as of the precedent term.

Michaelmas Term, 6 William IV, 1835.

14—*It is Ordered*, That in all cases, where application shall be made to a Judge in vacation after judgment by default, to make inquiry or assessment, under the Act of Assembly 5 Wm. IV, c. 37, s. 9, there shall be produced to the Judge a certificate or memorandum, of the day on which interlocutory judgment was signed, or judgment by default entered, signed by the Clerk of the Pleas or his deputy ; and that no such inquiry or assessment shall be made, unless such certificate or memorandum be so produced.

ATTACHMENT.

Hilary Term, 15 Victoria, 1852.

15—*It is Ordered*, That in future no attachment do issue unless taken out in the term during which the same may have been granted, or in the vacation next succeeding the same, without the order of the Court, or a Judge.

See No. 150.

ATTORNEYS.

Hilary Term, 60 George III, 1820.

16—*It is Ordered*, That in future, no Attorney of the Court, not being an established resident within the Province, be permitted to act as an Attorney of this Court.

ATTORNEYS, BARRISTERS AND STUDENTS— (ADMISSION OF.)

Hilary Term, 4 George IV, 1823.

17—1st. *It is Ordered*, That hereafter, no person, who'shall study the Law in this Province for the purpose of being admitted an Attorney of this Court, shall be so admitted unless he shall have so studied with some Barrister of this Court for the term of four years, if he be a Graduate of any College, or if not such Graduate, for the term of five years : *Provided*, That this Rule shall not extend to any person who shall have commenced his studies under any Barrister of this Court before the commencement of the present Term.

2nd. That no person producing a Certificate of admission as an Attorney of the Supreme Court of any other Province, Colony, or Island, in His Majesty's dominions, in order to obtain admission and enrollment as an Attorney of this Court, shall be so admitted and enrolled, unless he shall have served a regular Apprenticeship in such Province, Colony, or Island, agreeably to the terms prescribed in the foregoing rule for Students at Law in this Province, nor unless he shall produce an authenticated copy of the Certificate of such service, by virtue of which he may have obtained admission as an Attorney of the

Supreme Court of such Province, Colony, or Island, nor unless such Certificate shall include the qualifications as to age and moral character requisite in that behalf to be included in Certificates of service as Apprentices to the Law in this Province.

3rd. That after the expiration of two years from the time of admission as Attorneys, such Attorneys may be called to the Bar, provided there appears no just cause to prevent such call.

4th. That no person, admitted as an Attorney of this Court, shall, until he be called to the degree of a Barrister, be permitted to wear a Gown, or to make any motion as Counsel in any cause in this Court.

5th. That notice of every application, for admission as an Attorney of this Court, be filed with the Clerk of the Pleas on the first day of the Term at which such application may be made.

6th. That no person, under the degree of a Barrister, be hereafter entitled to take a Student for admission as an Attorney.

7th. That every Barrister taking a Student for admission as an Attorney, shall enter the name of such Student forthwith, with the Clerk of/the Pleas of this Court, to be enrolled by him in a Roll to be kept for that purpose, with the date of the commencement of such Student's term of study.

8th. That no Student, in any Barrister's office, shall be permitted hereafter to practice in the name of any Attorney, or otherwise, in any Inferior Court of Common Pleas in this Province.

Hilary Term, 6 George IV, 1825.

18—*Ordered,* That whenever any Attorney of this Court shall be desirous of being called to the Bar as Barrister, he shall make known his wishes, by petition to the Court, on the first day of the Term—which Petition shall be delivered to the Clerk, and be open for the inspection of Gentlemen of the Bar, until the sitting of the Court on Thursday following in the same term, when the Court will determine upon the said Petition.

Michaelmas Term, 6 William IV, 1835.

19—*It is Ordered,* That any Attorney, who, on his being admitted an Attorney, was a Graduate of any College, may be called to the Bar after the expiration of one year from the time of his admission as an Attorney.

Michaelmas Term, 1 Victoria, 1837.

20—1st. *Whereas* it is expedient, That every person desirous of being admitted as an Attorney of this Court should, before such admission, be examined as to his fitness and capacity to act as such Attorney; *It is Ordered,* That the Judges of this Court, together with four Barristers of not less than five years standing, to be for that purpose appointed by rule of Court in Hilary Term in every year, or any two of them, whereof a Judge to be one, shall be competent to conduct the examination of any person who may have made application for admission as an Attorney of this Court in the form hereafter mentioned; and that from and after the last day of next Hilary Term, subject to such appeal as hereafter mentioned, no person shall be admitted to be sworn as an Attorney of this Court without the production of a certificate signed by such examiners, testifying his fitness and capacity to act as an Attorney.

2nd. *It is Ordered,* That the said examination shall be held at such times and places respectively, and under such regulations as the Judges, or any three of them, may from time to time appoint.

3rd. That in case any person shall be dissatisfied with the refusal of the examiners to grant such certificate, he shall be at liberty to apply for admission, by petition in writing to the Judges: which application shall be heard by not less than three of the Judges, at such time and place as they may appoint.

4th. That every person who may desire to be admitted an Attorney shall, on or before the Thursday in the first week of the term immediately preceding that at which he shall propose to be admitted, make application by Petition to the Court, in the form hereunto annexed, or to the like effect, which petition shall be accompanied by the requisite certificates of the age, moral character, and service of the applicant; and the certificate of moral character shall be full, positive and explicit, and shall contain particular testimonials to the sober and temperate habits of the applicant, and the Court, if satisfied with the certificate, will, during such term, make order for the examination of such applicant.

5th. That the foregoing rules touching examination, shall extend to persons who may apply for admission upon certificates from any other part of Her Majesty's dominions, as well as to persons who may have pursued their studies in this Province; and any person coming from any other part of Her Majesty's dominions shall produce a certificate from the Court in which he may have become a practitioner, or one of the Judges thereof, that he has conducted himself with credit and reputation since his admission there.

6th. That no Attorney of this Court, who shall have been absent from the Province, or have discontinued the practice of the Law for the space of five years together, shall hereafter be permitted to commence or resume practice as an Attorney until he be re-admitted and re-sworn.

7th. That every Attorney, who may desire to be re-admitted, shall apply by petition to the Court, stating therein the place or places in which he may have resided, and the business, profession or employment in which he may have been engaged or concerned since his first admission; which petition shall be verified by the affidavit of the petitioner, and shall be presented to the Court on or before the Thursday in the first week of the term, immediately preceding that at which he may desire to be re-admitted.

8th. That every applicant for re-admission shall be examined as to his fitness and capacity to act as an Attorney, in the same manner as if applying for a first admission, unless the Court shall see fit in any case to dispense with such examination, and shall make order accordingly.

9th. That, from and after the present Michaelmas Term, no Attorney of any other part of Her Majesty's dominions shall be admitted as an Attorney of this Court, unless he shall have entered as a Student with one of the Attorneys of this Court, having the rank of Barrister, and resident and practising in the Province, and shall have continued as such Student for one year; the entry of every such Student to be registered with the Clerk, as in the case of other Students; and a certificate of such year's study from the Barrister with whom the same may have been performed shall be one of the testimonials necessary for the admission of such applicant.

Form of Petition for Admission as an Attorney.

To the Honorable the Chief Justice and Justices of the Supreme Court:

The Petition of A. B.   humbly sheweth, That your petitioner was born in   on   [state the place and day of birth], as by the accompanying certificate (or affidavit) will appear. That on   he entered as a Student in the office of C. D., Esquire, a Barrister of this Court, at   , in this Province, and has continued as such from that time hitherto; during which time he has not absented himself without the permission of the said C. D., nor been engaged in any other profession, business or employment.

[If the applicant have studied part of the time with any other Barrister, or been absent without permission, or engaged in any other profession, business or employment, since commencing his studies, he must state fully the reasons therefor, the particular time and length of such other study, or absence, or engagements in other pursuits, together with such other particulars as he may think advisable, explanatory of his conduct. If the applicant have not studied in this Province, he must state the particular grounds on which he applies for admission, the place or places in which he may have resided and practiced since his admission by any other Court; and, if he have been engaged in any other profession, business or employment, he must state the particulars of the same, with any other matters explanatory of his conduct and pursuits as he may deem necessary or advisable.*]

That your petitioner is at present resident at   and is desirous of being admitted an Attorney of this Honorable Court at the ensuing Term, and prays that your Honors will make such order touching his examination or admission as by the rules of the Court are required, or as to your Honors may seem meet. Dated the   day of   18

---

* If the petitioner's full time of study has not expired at the time of application, he must further state his intention to continue a Student in the Barrister's office until such time expires, and will be required to produce an additional certificate to that effect at the ensuing term.

Michaelmas Term, 4 Victoria, 1840.

21—1st. *It is Ordered,* That any Attorney who may before his admission have been an Attorney of some other part of Her Majesty's Dominions, and who shall have been a Student in this Province for one year pursuant to the ninth Rule of Michaelmas Term, 1st Victoria, may be called to the Bar after the expiration of one year from the time of his admission as an Attorney of this Court.

2nd. *It is Ordered,* That the admission and enrollment of Attorneys may take place on the Thursday in the first week of the Term, if there is no sufficient objection to the applicant.

Trinity Term, 5 Victoria, 1842.

22—*It is Ordered,* That Students, applying for examination after four years' study, on the ground of being Graduates of some College, do in addition to the certificates now required, produce certificates from the President, Vice-President, or some resident Professor of the College, stating the particular period during which their Collegiate studies have been pursued.

Trinity Term, 6 Victoria, 1843.

23—1st. *Whereas* it is expedient that there should be an examination of persons who may hereafter desire to enter upon the study of the Law, in order to their admission as Attorneys of this Court; *It is Ordered,* That such and so many Barristers as may for that purpose from time to time be appointed by rule of Court, or any two of them shall be competent to conduct the examination of any person who may have made application to be admitted a Student; and in order to such examination, application shall be made by petition to this Court by such person, stating his age, place of birth, and present residence; the name and place of residence of his father or guardian, and the several branches of education in which he may have been instructed; and that proper certificates as to character and habits shall accompany every such petition; and this Court will thereupon make such order for the examination or otherwise, as may appear necessary and proper.

2nd. That no entry shall be made in the Clerk's book of any Student, nor shall he be deemed to have commenced his study of the Law with any Barrister, until he produce the certificate of the examiners before whom his examination may be had, testifying his fitness and capacity.

3rd. That in case any person shall be dissatisfied with the refusal of the examiners to grant such certificate, he shall be at liberty to apply, by petition, to the Judges, who will make such order thereupon as the case may in their opinion require.

4th. That every Student, who may be transferred from one Barrister to another, during the progress of his studies, shall forthwith deliver to the Clerk a memorandum of such transfer, accompanied by a certificate of the Barrister whose office he may be desirous of leaving; or in case

2

of his death, absence, or refusal to grant such certificate, the certificate of the Barrister to whose office he is transferred, of the cause and reason of such transfer.

5th. That the aforegoing rules shall not extend to persons who may already have been admitted as Attorneys in any other part of Her Majesty's Dominions; but that such persons before being registered as Students under the ninth rule of Michaelmas Term, 1 Vic., shall apply, by petition, to the Court, accompanied by the requisite certificates; and the Court will make order thereupon.

6th. That if any person, who may, after his commencing to study the Law, have discontinued the same, shall be desirous of resuming his studies, he shall apply, by petition, to the Court for that purpose, who will make such order thereupon in regard to the time of his previous study, as may appear meet; otherwise the time of such former study shall not be allowed to such Student.

Michaelmas Term, 11 Victoria, 1847.

24—*Whereas* certain rules and regulations, touching the examination of persons as Students-at-Law, and Attorneys, and the admission of Attorneys and Barristers of the Supreme Court, were duly made by the Barristers' Society in Hilary Term last, at a meeting of the said Society holden at Fredericton, pursuant to the Act of Assembly, 9th Vic. c. 49, which said rules and regulations have been sanctioned by the Judges of this Court, in conformity to the said Act, and are as follows:—

" At a meeting of the Barristers' Society of New Brunswick, holden in the Supreme Court Room, at Fredericton, this 8th day of February, A.D. 1874, the following rules were adopted :—

RULES TOUCHING THE EXAMINATION OF PERSONS AS STUDENTS-AT-LAW AND ATTORNEYS, AND REGULATING THE ADMISSION OF ATTORNEYS AND BARRISTERS OF THE SUPREME COURT.

" I. That before any person is presented to the Barristers' Society for the purpose of being examined, in order to his being entered as a Student in the Office of any Barrister of this Society, he shall present a Petition to the Benchers, setting forth his age, place of birth, residence, place of education, the branches in which he is prepared to undergo an examination, and the name of the Barrister with whom he purposes studying; which Petition shall be subscribed by the applicant, and certified by such Barrister, as to his character and habits, and that he verily believes him to be a proper person to be admitted as a Student-at-Law; and upon such applicant being approved of by the Benchers, he shall be fully and strictly examined in the English and Latin Languages, Mathematics, Geography and History, by the said Benchers, or any three of them at Fredericton.

"II. That upon the applicant passing such examination, and the Benchers being satisfied as to his moral character, good habits, and fitness to enter upon the study of the Law, he shall receive a certificate to that effect

"III. That every Student making application for admission as an Attorney, shall give a Term's notice thereof to the Society, and shall undergo a full and strict examination before the Benchers, or any three of them, in the Elementary principles of the Law of Real and Personal Property, Forms of Action, Pleading, Evidence and Practice.

"IV. That upon the Student passing such examination, and the Benchers being fully satisfied as to his moral character, habits and conduct during the term of his study, he shall be recommended for admission as an Attorney; provided always, that in case any Student shall not pass his examination before three of the Benchers as aforesaid, such Benchers shall report the fact to the whole body of Benchers, and he may be heard before them against the refusal of his certificate.

"V. That every Attorney applying to be called to the Bar, shall give to this Society a Term's notice of such his intention; and if, during the period since his admission as an Attorney, his practice and conduct have been professional and honorable, and no objections are made to his moral character and habits. he shall be recommended accordingly: but if objections be made, an enquiry therein shall be instituted by the Benchers, or a Committee of them; and upon such inquiry, the said Benchers, or a Committee as aforesaid, shall either grant or withhold a certificate of recommendation for such Attorney's admission as a Barrister, as to them may appear just and right in the premises."

FURTHER REGULATIONS BY BARRISTERS' SOCIETY, PASSED 8TH FEBRUARY, 1867.

Before any person is presented to the Barrister' Society, for the purpose of being examined, in order to his being entered as a Student in the office of any Barrister, he shall give a Term's previous notice in writing put up in the Library Room, on or before the first Friday of the Term, and shall present a Petition to the Council of the said Society. setting forth his age, place of birth, residence, place of education, the branches in which he is prepared to undergo an examination, and the name of the Barrister with whom he proposes to study, which petition shall be subscribed by the applicant, and certified by such Barrister, after a careful enquiry and personal examination, as to the character, habits and education of the applicant, and that upon such enquiry and examination, the Barrister verily believes the applicant to be a proper person and properly qualified to be admitted as a Student-at-Law, and upon his being approved by the Council, he shall be fully examined at Fredericton, at such time as may be appointed, by questions in writing, in such branches as two members of the Council (one being an examiner) may determine, subject to the approval of a Judge, and who shall certify accordingly.

Upon the applicant passing such examination, and the Council being satisfied as to his moral character, good habits, and fitness to enter on the study of the Law, he shall receive a certificate to that effect.

Every Student making application for admission, as an Attorney, shall give a Term's notice, by a writing for that purpose put up in the Law Library on or before the first Friday of the Term, and shall undergo an examination at such time and place as the Council or any two members thereof, (an examiner being one), may appoint, by written questions previously prepared, under the authority of the Council, who may alter, add to, or amend the same, for such Student or Students to answer, who shall put the answers to such questions in writing and during such examination shall not be permitted to refer to any book, or person, or other source of information, to assist him in such answers, and shall write the same in a legible hand, in the presence of one of the said Council, or the Secretary of the said Society, which written answers shall be submitted to the aforesaid two members of Council for their opinion upon the same, who, after examination, shall submit them for the approval of one of the Judges, such answers to be so submitted and decided on, without the said members or Judge knowing the name of the respective parties who gave in the same, such answers being designated by letters or numbers only ; and if such Student shall be deemed qualified, he shall receive a first, second or third class certificate, according to the merits of his written answers.

That upon a Student passing such examination, and the Council being fully satisfied as to his moral character, habits and conduct during the term of his study, he shall be recommended for admission as an Attorney.

And whereas it is highly necessary, as well for the interest of every person entering upon the study of the Law, as for " securing to the Province and the Profession, a learned and honorable body,' especially in the late curtailed period of study, that students of the Law, during their Studentship, should confine themselves exclusively to the study of their profession, and not receive any emolument or reward for their services, or engage in any other profession, business, or employment : No Student, therefore, shall receive any salary or remuneration whatever for his services from the Barrister with whom he studies, nor from any other person, nor shall he be allowed to practice or try causes in any Court, on pain of being refused admission.

Every Attorney applying to be called to the Bar shall give to this Society, a Term's notice of such his intention, and if during the period since his admission as an Attorney, his practice and conduct have been professionable and honorable, and no objections are made to his moral character and habits, he shall be recommended accordingly, but, if objections be made, an enquiry therein shall be instituted by the Council, and upon such enquiry the said Council shall either grant or withhold a certificate of recommendation for such Attorney's admission, as Barrister, as to them may appear just and right in the premises, subject to appeal as aforesaid.

Michaelmas Term; 42 Victoria, 1879.

Admission of Attorneys.

25—Whenever any Attorney intending to apply for admission as a Barrister or any Student intending to apply for admission as an Attorney, shall have been recommended for admission by the Barrister's Society, pursuant to the Rules of Court of Michaelmas Term·1847 ; such recommendation, together, with the necessary Certificates of moral character and term of study, shall be delivered to the Court on the day preceeding that on which it is intended to move for their admission ; and if the Certificates, etc., are satisfactory, the applicants may be admitted at the opening of the Court on the following day.

(See No. 136.)

Easter Term, 19 Victoria, 1856.

26—*It is Ordered*, That any Barrister of the Supreme or Superior Court or Courts of any of Her Majesty's Colonies or Possessions in North America, Bermuda, or the West Indies, and entitled to practice as such in all the Supreme Courts of that Colony or Possession in which he may have been originally admitted a Barrister, may, upon the recommendation of the Barristers' Society, be called, sworn, and enrolled a Barrister of this Court, and entitled to the rights and privileges as such so long as he shall be a member of the said Barristers' Society ; provided always, that no such Barrister of any other British Colony or Possession shall be entitled to be admitted a Barrister of this Court, unless it be proved to the satisfaction of this Court, that a Barrister of this Court would be entitled to like rights and privileges in all the Superior Courts of that Colony or Possession in which the applicant may have been originally admitted a Barrister.

Hilary Term, 21 Victoria, 1858.

27—*It is Ordered*, That the privilege granted by the Rule of Court to Students applying for admission as Attorneys, and to Attorneys applying for admission as Barristers, when such Students and Attorneys are Graduates of some College or University, be confined to Graduates of some University situate within the British Dominions ; but that such order shall not apply to any Student already entered.

Examination. See No. 136.

See Acts of Assembly 26 Vic. (1866), cap. 23, limiting term of study.

AWARDS AND WARRANTS OF ATTORNEY.

Michaelmas Term, 6 William IV, 1835.

28—*It is Ordered*, That when a rule to shew cause is obtained to set aside an award or Warrant of Attorney, or a judgment entered upon an Award or Warrant of Attorney, the several objections, intended to be insisted upon at the time of making such rule absolute, shall be stated in the rule to shew cause.

Hilary Term, 7 William IV, 1837.

29—1st. *It is Ordered*, That no judgment be signed upon any Warrant authorising any Attorney to confess judgment without such Warrant being delivered to, and filed by the Clerk.

2nd. *It is Ordered*, That every Attorney of this Court who shall prepare any Warrant of Attorney to confess any judgment which is to be subject to any defeasance, do cause such defeasance to be written on the same paper or parchment on which the Warrant of Attorney shall be written, or cause a memorandum in writing to be made on such Warrant, containing the substance and effect of such defeasance.

3rd. *It is Ordered*, That no Sheriff, Bailiff, or Sheriff's Officer, shall presume to exact or take from any person or persons being in his custody by arrest, any Warrant to confess judgment, but in the presence of an Attorney for the Defendant, which Attorney shall then subscribe his name thereto ; and that no Attorney do acknowledge or enter any judgment by color of any Warrant given by any Defendant being under arrest, otherwise than is aforesaid.

Easter Term, 11 Victoria, 1848.

30—No Judgment to be signed on a Warrant of Attorney after one year from its date without the order of the Court, or of a Judge.

Trinity Term, 20 Victoria, 1857.

31—1st. *It is Ordered*, That in no case where the Warrant of Attorney to confess judgment appears to have been executed, not personally, but by an Attorney or Agent in the name of the principal, shall any confession be signed thereon by an Attorney of this Court, unless the deed or other power conveying the authority to execute the Warrant, together with an affidavit of the due execution thereof by the principal, be produced to, and read and examined by the Attorney who is applied to, to sign the confession, before signing the same; nor shall judgment be entered upon any such confession unless such deed or other power, and affidavit of execution, be produced to the Clerk, and filed with the Warrant of Attorney and confession.

2nd. *It is further Ordered*, That if such deed or other power bear date or appear to have been given more than a year and a day before the application to sign judgment, no judgment be entered thereupon without the order of a Judge, nor after ten years without a rule of Court founded on a previous rule *nisi*, as is now the practice in regard to Warrants of Attorney of those respective dates.

3rd. *It is further Ordered*, That every Warrant of Attorney to confess judgment; and every deed or other power by which authority is granted to execute the Warrant, bear date of the day upon which the same are respectively executed; and if it should happen that such Warrant of Attorney, deed, or other power, is to be given by two or more persons who cannot conveniently execute the same on the same day, then the warrant, deed, or power, shall bear date of the day cn which it shall be first executed; and the day on which any subsequent execution shall take place shall be specified in the attestation of the subscribing witness or witnesses to such execution.

4th. *It is further Ordered*, That every Attorney signing a confession of judgment upon a Warrant of Attorney, do annex to his signature the date of signing, and do mark with his name, or initial letters of his name, the said Warrant of Attorney, and also any deed or power under which the Warrant is executed, where the execution is not personal.

Barristers. See Attorneys, etc.

Bail. See Special Bail.

BILL OF PARTICULARS.

Hilary Term, 6 William IV, 1836.

32—*It is Ordered*, That a copy of the Bill of Particulars of the Plaintiff's demand, and also of the Defendant's set-off (if any) shall be filed by the Plaintiff's Attorney, with every record of *Nisi Prius*, at the time of entering the same.

BILL AND TAXATION OF COSTS.

Michaelmas Term, 40 George III, 1800.

33—*Ordered*, That every Attorney of this Court deliver a regular bill of costs to his Client, or to the Client of the adverse Attorney, as the case may be, before he demands the expenses of the suit; and all receipts by Attorneys from their Clients, without this previous step, will be considered as a breach of this Rule.

Easter Term, 12 Victoria, 1849.

34—*It is Ordered*, That the following Regulations be observed in the Office of the Clerk of the Pleas:

1st. Every affidavit used before the Clerk, on the taxation of costs, to be retained and filed on a file to be kept for this purpose.

2nd. The names of witnesses, the days attendance and mileage of each witness, to be specified in every Bill of Costs, brought for taxation.

BLANK WRITS.

See Records, etc.

CALCULATING INTEREST.

Hilary Term, 2 George IV, 1821.

35—Interest upon Bonds, Debts, and other Securities for money, payable with interest, should be ascertained by adding the Interest to the principal at the time of each payment, and deducting the payment, which is the same thing as first deducting the Interest from the payment, and then giving credit for the balance on account of principal ; and not by charging Interest upon the whole Bond to the time of the last payment, and Interest for the Debtor on the several payments from their respective dates, thereby inverting the principle of compound Interest, and charging Interest on his own debts, when a payment is made of less than the Interest due at the time. Nothing should be credited until a sum is paid equal to the Interest then due, except by endorsing it specially as a sum paid in part of the Interest then due.

CLERK OF PLEAS.

36—Regulation to be observed in office of. See Nos. 30, 34, 37, 54, 60, 71, 96, 104.

CONFESSION OF JUDGMENT.
Easter Term, 11 Victoria, 1848.

37—No Judgment to be signed upon any confession, cognovit, or retraxit, after one year from the date thereof, or from the Term whereof the same is granted, without the order of the Court, or of a Judge.

CONSENT RULE.

See Rule (Consent.)

COSTS—TAXATION.

See Bill and Taxation—Security for Costs.

COUNTY COURT APPEALS.

See Appeal Paper No. 9.

CROWN CASES RESERVED.
Michaelmas Term, 40 Victoria, 1876.

38—*It is Ordered*, That cases reserved for the opinion of the Supreme Court, under the Revised Statutes, Chapter 159, Section 22, shall come on to be heard immediately after the conclusion of the motions for new trial.

CROWN OFFICE.

Regulations to be observed. See Nos. 111, 150.

CROWN PAPER.

See Special Paper.

DAMAGES (ASSESSMENT OF.)

See No. 13.

Damages—Interest on—Form of entry of Judgment. See No. 57.

DEED—PROOF OF EXECUTION.

See Subpœna.

DECLARATIONS.

Easter Term, 25 George III, 1785.

39—That all Attorneys file their Declarations on or before the last day of the Term next enusing the return and filing the Writ, or be *non prossed.*

Easter Term, 26 George III, 1786.

40—*It is Ordered,* That upon all Process where no Affidavit is made or filed of the cause of action, the Plaintiff may file or deliver the Declaration *De Bene Esse* at the return of such Process, with notice to plead in twenty days; and if Defendant doth not enter an appearance or file common Bail, and plead within the said twenty days, Plaintiff having first filed common Bail for Defendant, may sign Judgment for want of a Plea, provided that such Declaration be delivered or filed in the Clerk's Office with notice thereon, within *twenty* days after the return of such Process. and a rule to plead be duly entered.

Michaelmas Term, 6 George IV, 1825.

41—*It is Ordered,* That the time for delivering or filing Declarations *De Bene Esse,* agreeably to the rule made in Easter Term in the 26th George III, be enlarged to thirty days.

DEFAULT—NON PROS—JUDGMENT.

Hilary Term, 6 William IV, 1836.

42—*It is Ordered,* That no Judgment of *Non Pros* shall be signed for want of a declaration, replication, or other subsequent pleading, until ten days next after a demand thereof shall have been made in writing upon the Plaintiff, his Attorney, or Agent, as the case may be.

Hilary Term, 2 Victoria, 1839.

43—1st. *Ordered,* That in future where the Defendant in any action shall plead one or more special pleas, and serve copies on the Plaintiff's Attorney, with rule to reply in twenty days, the Plaintiff shall file and deliver his replication in twenty days from the time of such service of plea and rule, and in default thereof the Defendant shall be entitled to judgment of *Non Pros,* a replication being first demanded after the said twenty days; and in like manner twenty days shall be allowed for every subsequent pleading, and the opposite party shall be entitled to judgment by default or *Non Pros,* as the case may be, for not rejoining, surrejoining, etc., a rule to rejoin, surrejoin, etc., being served and

3

demand made as aforesaid, unless the Ccurt or a Judge shall think proper to allow further time. Provided that no such judgment of *Non Pros* or default shall be signed until ten days after demand of replication, rejoinder, etc.

2nd. That all such rules to reply, rejoin, surrejoin, etc., may be taken out in vacation and entered as of the preceding term, the Attorney delivering to the Clerk a præcipe for such rule.

DELIVERY CF PLEAS.

See Pleas.

DEMAND OF PLEAS.

See Pleas.

DEMURRER AND SPECIAL CASES.
Trinity Term, 3 Victoria, 1840.

44—*It is further Ordered,* That where a general Demurrer shall hereafter be put in to any Declaration or other pleading, the party putting in the same shall deliver at the same time to the opposite party a statement or minute of the grounds of such Demurrer; and if the opposite party intend to rely on any defects in the previous pleading, he shall deliver with the joinder in demurrer a statement or minute of such alleged defects; and such particulars shall be entered in the margin of the books delivered to the Judges. This regulation to extend also to cases of Special Demurrer where other grounds are intended to be relied on, than those specifically set out.

Hilary Term, 9 Victoria, 1846.

45—*Ordered,* That twenty days from the delivery of a copy of any demurrer, shall be allowed to the opposite party to join in demurrer, and furnish a note of objections to the previous pleading, (if any) agreeably to the rule of Trinity Term, 3 Vic,; on failure of which, the joinder in demurrer may be added by the party demurring, in making up the demurrer book; and no copy of such demurrer book need be served on the opposite Attorney, nor shall any motion or rule for a concilium be required; but demurrers, as well as special cases and special verdicts, shall be entered for argument at the request of either party, of which notice shall be given to the opposite Attorney eight days before the term at which such entry is made.

Trinity Term, 31 Victoria, 1868.

46—All special cases submitted for the opinion of the Supreme Court, —either on the Equity or Pleas side,—shall be printed at the joint expense of both parties, and copies thereof furnished for the use of the

Judges and for the Clerk of the Court, and the cost thereof shall be taxed and allowed after the decision of the case according to the rights of the parties.

DEMURRER BOOKS.

Trinity Term, 2 William IV, 1831.

47—*Whereas* expense is often unnecessarily incurred in making up Demurrer Books, from setting forth those parts of the pleadings to which the Demurrers do not apply. *It is therefor Ordered*, That from and after the end of this Term, when there shall be a demurrer to part only of the declaration or other subsequent pleadings, those parts only of the declaration and pleadings to which such demurrer relates shall be copied into the Demurrer Book; and, if any other parts shall be copied, the Clerk shall not allow the costs thereof on taxation, either as between party and party, or as between Attorney and Client.

Hilary Term, 6 William IV, 1836.

48—*It is Ordered*, That Demurrer Books be delivered to the Judges on cr before the first day of the term at which the Demurrer is to be argued, the books for the Chief Justice and senior Puisne Judge to be prepared and delivered by the Plaintiff's Attorney, and the books for the two junior Judges by the Defendant's Attorney; and that the same rule do also apply to other cases in which paper books are required by the practice of the Court to be delivered to the Judges.

Michaelmas Term, 9 Victoria, 1845.

49—*Ordered*, That if either party make default in the delivery of the demurrer books, as required by the rule of Hilary Term, 6 Wm. IV, the other party who has complied with the rule may move for judgment without having delivered books to all the Judges.

DIVORCE AND MATRIMONIAL CAUSES.

See Appeal Papers Nos. 9, 10 & 11.

Hilary Term, 26 Victoria, 1863.

50—1st. *It is Ordered*, That the Clerk of the Pleas do keep a Paper, to be called the Divorce and Matrimonial Appeal Paper, in which shall be entered all Appeals from decisions of the Court of Divorce and Matrimonial causes ; such entries to be made on or before the first day of the Term next after the decisions in the said Court; such appeals to be heard next after the Equity appeal paper.

2nd. *It is Ordered*, That upon hearing of an appeal from the Court of Divorce and Matrimonial Causes, pursuant to the Act of Assembly, 23rd Victoria, cap. 37, it shall be the duty of the appellant to procure and file with the Clerk of the Pleas in this Court, certified copies of the libel and answer and Decree ; and that on hearing the appeal, the evidence be received from the Report of the Judge of the Court of Divorce and Matrimonial Causes.

DOCKETS.

See Records, etc.

EJECTMENT.

Michaelmas Term, 6 William IV, 1835.

51—1st. *It is Ordered*, That in all actions of ejectment, the notice to appear may be for any return day specifically, but when the notice to appear is for the term generally, the day of appearance shall be the first day of the term.

    2nd. *It is Ordered*, That in all actions of ejectment, there shall be fourteen days exclusive between the day of serving the declaration and the day of appearance, whether the person served with the declaration lives within the County where the Court sits or not, any former Rule to the contrary notwithstanding.

Trinity Term, 6 William IV, 1836.

52—*It is Ordered*, That the notice to appear in ejectment, shall not be made in future for the return day in the second week of the term; but for the term generally, or the Tuesday or Saturday in the first week.

    Consent Rules. (See Nos. 115, 116.)

ENTRY OF CAUSE IN CLERK'S OFFICE.

53—See Appeal Paper, Nos. 9, 10 & 11. See Rules 44, 45.

Easter Term, 11 Victoria, 1848.

Entry of Cause. See Nos. 9, 10 & 11.

54—No Judgment. interlocutory or final, to be signed in any cause until it is ascertained, upon search,, that the cause has been duly entered ; provided, that where there is an interlocutory judgment, the search need not be repeated when final judgment is signed ; and provided also, that entries may be made as heretofore accustomed in case of warrants of Attorney to confess judgment.

ENTRY FOR HEARING AT SITTINGS IN EQUITY.

Trinity Term, 31 Victoria, 1868.

55—All causes intended for hearing at the Sittings in Equity, shall be set down with the Clerk in Equity six days before the first day of the Sitting of the Court, and shall be entered by him on a Docket to be kept for that purpose, and no cause not so entered shall be heard without the order of the Judge sitting in such Court.

Entry of cause for argument. See Appeal Paper—Motion Paper.

Entry of Cause—Equity Appeal Paper. See Appeal Paper Nos. 9, 10 & 11.

Michaelmas Term, 19 Victoria, 1855.

56—*It is Ordered*, That a Paper be prepared by the Clerk of the Court on the Equity side, and delivered to the Court on the first day of each Term, containing a List of the Causes in Equity in which appeals are to be heard, which shall be called the Equity Appeal Paper, and the Causes therein shall come on to be heard in order next after the Special Paper of the same Term.

ENTRY ON JUDGMENT ROLL—INTEREST ON DAMAGES.

Michaelmas Term, 20 Victoria, 1856.

57—*It is Ordered*, That where interest is awarded under the Act of Assembly 12th Victoria, cap. 39, sec. 29, the entry on the Judgment roll shall be in the form following, or to the like effect:

"Therefore it is considered that the said plaintiff do recover against the said defendant, etc., etc., etc., together with —— now adjudged by the Court here to the said plaintiff for interest upon the damages (*or* debt) pursuant to the Act of Assembly in such case made and provided, because the final judgment has been delayed by the act of the defendant; and also—— for his costs and charges, etc., etc., etc., which said damages, interest, costs, and charges, amount in the whole to——."

Equity Appeal Paper. See Appeal Paper Nos. 9, 10 & 11.

Equity—Service on Non-residents. See Practice in Equity.

EXAMINING WITNESSES UPON INTERROGATORIES.

Hilary Term, 7 William IV, 1837.

58—*It is Ordered*, That the party applying for the examination of a witness or witnesses *de bene esse*, under the Act 26 George III, c. 20, or for an order for such examination, or for the issuing a commission, under the Act 5 Wm. IV, c. 34, do state in the affidavit or affidavits upon which such application is founded, the nature of the action, the venue, and the state of the pleadings or proceedings at the time of such application; also the name of the opposite Attorney or Agent; and do also, whenever time will permit, give notice of such application, together with a copy of the affidavit or affidavits, to such Attorney or Agent.

FEES AND FORMS.

Easter Term, 1875.

59—*It is Ordered,* That the table of Fees and Forms prescribed on the 31st day of October last, únder the Act of Assembly 37 Vic., cap. 7 :
" To provide for process of Attachment in certain civil suits, and to abolish Imprisonment for Debt, together with the table of Fees under "The Common Law procedure Act", 1873, shall, as far as may be applicable, be used, taken and allowed, under the Act 38 Victoria, cap. 4, entitled, " An Act to amend the Attachment and Abolition of Imprisonment for Debt Act", and under the Act 38 Vic., cap. 5, entitled, "An Act to provide for Garnishee or Trustee Process," until the same be altered under the authority given by the said last mentioned Acts."

Easter Term, 40 Victoria, 1876.

ATTACHMENT AND ABOLITION OF IMPRISONMENT ACT—GARNISHEE PROCESS.

59 a—In pursuance of the powers given by the Acts of Assembly 38 Vic., c. 4, entitled " An Act to amend the attachment and abolition of imprisonment for Debt Act," and 38 Victoria, cap. 5, entitled " An Act to provide for Garnishee or Trustee Process," the following Table of Fees has been fixed and ordained by the Supreme Court to be taken in proceedings under the said Acts :

Order to bring up a confined debtor for disclosure	$0 50
Holding examination	1 00
Taking minutes of the same, per folio	0 20
Adjournment, when necessary	0 50
Order for discharge or to remand	0 50
Attaching order	1 00
Every other order	0 50
Order for the examination of a Primary or Judgment Debtor, under 38 Vic., c. 4, s. 25	1 00
Holding examination	2 00
Taking the minutes when required, per folio	0 20
Garnishee, or other Summons	0 50
Hearing on Garnishee Summons, or Order	2 00
Taking minutes, per folio	0 20
Examining and taxing costs	0 30

To the Sheriff or Gaoler.

Bringing a debtor for disclosure	0 60

For executing a Writ of Attachment for disobedience of
Judge's order, or to a subpœna, the same fees as are
allowed for executing Writs out of the County Court.

FILING PAPERS OR RECORDS IN CLERK'S OFFICE.

Hilary Term, 1875.

60—Every record, or paper, to be filed in the office of the Clerk of the Pleas, shall be plainly and legibly endorsed with the title of the cause and the name of the Attorney filing the same, and shall be folded to a width of not less than two and a half inches. No record, or paper, substantially varying from-this regulation, shall be received by the Clerk.

FOREIGN JUDGMENT—HOLDING TO BAIL UPON.

Hilary Term, 26 Victoria, 1863.

61—*It is Ordered,* That no person shall be held to bail upon the Judgment of the Court of any Foreign Country, or of any British Colony, without a Judge's order.

GRADUATE'S CERTIFICATE.

See Attorneys, Barristers, etc:

HEARING CAUSES—ENTRY.

See Appeal Paper, No. 11, s. 4.

INFANTS—PROCEEDINGS AGAINST.

Trinity Term, 31 Victoria, 1868.

62—When any person residing out of the Province, against whom a suit is commenced, is an infant, and does not appear within the time limited by the order made for that purpose, under the Act 17 Vic., c. 18, s. 3, the Court may make the like order for the appearance of the infant, as is provided by the 12th rule of the 5th of July, 1853, (see Botsford Rules 23), and at the expiration of the time so limited, the plaintiff may proceed to prove his case against the infant in the manner provided by the said rule.

Interest—Calculation of—Mode. See No. 35.

Interest on Damages—Judgment form of. See No. 57.

Interrogatories—Examination on. See No. 58.

INTERLOCUTORY JUDGMENT.

Easter Term, 25 George III, 1785.

63—That on filing a Declaration in any action, the plaintiff be entitled to Judgment, if the defendant doth not plead in twenty days after notice of Declaration being filed in the Clerk's Office, the Rule to plead being first entered ; and if the defendant hath not entered his appearance in such action, the plaintiff may file a common appearance, and enter an Interlocutory Judgment for want of a Plea as of the preceding term, without any imparlance, and proceed to a Writ of Inquiry as if the same Interlocutory Judgment had been rendered and entered the same preceding Term ; and the like proceeding to entry of Judgment and executing Writ of Inquiry, where a defendant in custody neglects to plead, pursuant to a rule served on himself, or the Sheriff as aforesaid.

Trinity Term, 3 Victoria, 1840.

64—*It is Ordered,* That Interlocutory Judgment shall not be signed in any case for want of appearance until the process with the requisite affidavit of service, and (where the case requires) the order of the Court or Judge for perfecting such service, shall be filed.

Trinity Term, 20 Victoria, 1857.

65—*It is Ordered,* That from and after the present Term, in every Memorandum of Interlocutory Judgment, the Term at which the writ has been made returnable be specified on the margin or at the foot of the Memorandum, and that it be also stated whether the action is summary or not summary.

JUDGMENT AS IN CASE OF NON-SUIT.

Hilary Term, 6 William IV, 1836.

66—1st. *It is Ordered,* That no motion shall be made for Judgment, as in case of a non-suit, pursuant to the Statute 14 George II, c. 17, without notice having been first given thereof to the plaintiff, his Attorney or Agent, as the case may be, together with a copy of the affidavit on which the same is grounded, at least fourteen days before the term at which such motion is intended to be made, and without entering the same on the Motion Paper.

2nd. *It is Ordered,* That on motion made in open Court pursuant to the said entry, and on due proof of the service of notice and copy of affidavit as directed by the preceding rule, the defendant shall be entitled to a rule absolute for Judgment as in case of a non-suit, unless the Court on just cause and reasonable terms shall allow a further time for the trial of the issue, or unless the Court should think fit to enlarge the time for shewing cause to the next term.

Trinity Term, 12 Victoria, 1849.

67—*It is Ordered,* That in the notice of motion for Judgment, as in case of a non-suit, the copy of affidavit, as required by Rule 3, Hilary Term, 6 Wm. IV, shall be deemed sufficient if served on Tuesday, the fourteenth day preceding the Term, so as to make the notice of motion in this case conform to the other notices of motion upon the Motion Paper.

Michaelmas Term, 23 Victoria, 1859.

68—*It is Ordered*, That in future the affidavit on which motion is made for Judgment as in case of a non-suit for not proceeding to trial according to the practice of the Court, (where notice of trial has not been given,) do state the particular Term in or before which issue has been joined, or do state some particular day in vacation on or before which issue has been joined.

JUDGMENT IN DEBT.

Trinity Term, 1 Victoria, 1838.

69—*It is Ordered*, That the entry of the judgment on the record, in actions of debt, where the amount to be recovered, is ascertained and assessed by the Court, under the Act of Assembly, 7 Wm. IV, c. 14, s. 6, shall be in the following form, or of the like tenor and effect, viz.:

"And the said A. B. (*the Plaintiff*) prays that the amount to be recovered in this action, may be ascertained and assessed by the Court here, according to the form of the Act of Assembly, in such case made and provided; and thereupon it is suggested and proved, and manifestly appears to the Court here, that the said A. B. ought to recover for his debt in this action, the sum of £———; therefore it is considered that the said A. B. do recover against the said C. D. (*the Defendant*) the said sum of £———, for his debt, so ascertained and assessed by the Court here, and also, etc., (proceed with the entry in regard to costs, in the usual form,) and the said C. D. in mercy, etc.

JUDGMENT—DEFAULT—NON PROS.

See Nos. 42, 43.

JUDGMENT ROLLS.

See Records, Writs, etc.

Easter Term, 11 Victoria, 1848.

71—All Judgment Rolls to be endorsed with the title of the Term wherein final judgment is awarded ; and when judgment is entered in vacation, then to be endorsed of the Term next preceding, and the Rolls are to be numbered consecutively as they are brought in and filed of such Term, and to be referred to in pleading as the Rolls of such Term.

JUDGMENT ROLL ON OFFER TO SUFFER JUDGMENT BY DEFAULT.

Trinity Term, 22 Victoria, 1859.

72—*It is Ordered*, That in any case (not summary) where, under the provisions of the Act of Assembly, 18th Victoria, cap. 9, an offer and consent in writing has been filed by the defendant, to suffer judgment

4

by default, for a certain specified sum as debt or damages, (as the case may be) and the plaintiff has not, after due notice thereof, filed his acceptance of such offer, but has taken the case down to trial, and has recovered a verdict, but not for a greater sum than the sum so offered, the entry or suggestion on the Judgment Roll shall be as follows :—

" And now, pursuant to the Act of Assembly passed in the eighteenth year of the Reign of Queen Victoria, entitled, 'An Act concerning Tender in Actions at Law and Suits in Equity,' on the —— day of —— in the year of our Lord —— the said defendant C. D., files in the Office of the Clerk of the Pleas of this Court, an offer or consent in writing in the words following :— [*insert the offer*]—which offer and consent the said plaintiff A. B., has not accepted ; therefore the issue joined between the parties remains to be tried : Therefore let a jury thereupon come, etc." [*as in ordinary cases, to the conclusion of the postea,*] and then proceed as follows :—

" And inasmuch as it appears by the said return, that the debt [*or damages*] was not greater in amount than the sum for which the said C. D. offered to suffer judgment by default, it is considered that the said A. B. do recover his said debt [*or damages*] so assessed at the sum of ——, together with his costs and charges by him about his suit in this behalf expended, up to the said —— day of ——, and for these costs and charges to ——, which said debt, [*or damages*] costs and charges in the whole amount to ——, and that the said A. B. have execution thereof. And it is further considered that the said C. D. do recover against the said A. B. —— for his costs and charges by him incurred after the said —— day of ——. and that he have execution thereof."

(On interest on Damages. See 57.)

JUDGES' ORDERS.
Michaelmas Term, 42 Victoria, 1879.

73—Judge's Orders, and Orders of Nisi Prius, may be made Rules of Court on the production of Counsel's signature, without any motion for that purpose.

JUDGES' SUMMONS.
Hilary Term, 6 William IV, 1836.

74—*It is Ordered,* That it shall not be necessary to issue more than one summons for attendance before a Judge upon the same matter, and the party taking out such summons, shall, if the Judge see fit, be entitled to an order on the return of the summons, unless cause is shewn to the contrary.

JURY RETIRING TO CONSIDER VERDICT— ENTERING TIME.
Easter Term, 18 Victoria, 1855.

75—1st. The Clerk at any Circuit Court or Sittings, shall enter on the Minutes the time when the Jury retire to consider of their verdict, and also the time when the Jury return into Court to deliver their verdict.

2nd. If they return within two hours, the verdict shall be taken and entered in manner heretofore accustomed.

3rd. If they return after the lapse of two hours, after they are called over by their names and answer thereto, they shall be asked thus—Gentlemen of the Jury, are you all agreed on your verdict, or how many and which of you are agreed thereupon ?

If they shall answer that they are all agreed, the verdict shall be taken and entered in the usual manner. If they shall answer that they are not all agreed, but that five (*or* six) are agreed, the names of the Jurors by whom the verdict is so returned shall be taken and entered in the Minutes, and the verdict shall be recorded as follows :—

The Jury having considered of their verdict, and not being able all to agree within two hours, five (*or* six) of their number, namely, A. B., [*the names to be here specified,*] do say that they do find [*the finding to be here stated.*]

This entry shall then be read over to the Jury distinctly, and shall be returned on the Postea as follows :—

POSTEA.
[*Commencing in the ordinary form.*]

And the Jurors of that Jury being summoned also come, who to speak the truth of the matters within contained, are chosen, tried, and sworn, and having retired to consider of their verdict, and not being able to agreed within two hours, five (*or* six) of their number, namely, [*here set forth the names,*] pursuant to the Act of Assembly relating to Jurors, say upon their oath, [*here state the verdict.*]

Constable's Oath. See No. 95.

MESNE PROCESS.

Michaelmas Term, 6 William IV, 1835.

76—*It is Ordered,* That every mesne process, in any action, shall contain the names of all the Defendants, if more than one, in the action.

MONEYS PAID INTO COURT.

Statement of—Rules respecting. See Rules Nos. 154, 155.

MOTION DAY.

Michaelmas Term, 29 Victoria, 1865.

77—*It is Ordered,* That Tuesday in the second week of each Term shall be the regular day for motions, instead of Saturday of that week ; on which day, motions shall have the precedence of the ordinary business, which however shall be proceeded with after the motions are concluded ;—

Provided, however, that one or more of the Judges will sit in Court
on the second Saturday, whenever occasion may require.

Hilary Term, 40 Victoria, 1877.

78—*It is Ordered*, That the Rule of Michaelmas Term, 29th Victoria, which
provides that "Tuesday in the second week in each Term shall be the
regular day for motions, instead of Saturday of that week," is hereby
rescinded; and that the second Saturday in each Term shall be a day
for such motions.

MOTION PAPER.

Hilary Term, 6 William IV, 1836.

79—1st. *It is Ordered*, That in future the Clerk of the Pleas do keep a
paper, to be called the Motion Paper, in which shall be entered all
motions of which notice may have been given, such entries to be made
on or before the first day of each Term, and to stand in the said paper
in the order in which they may be made, and the matters contained in
such Motion Paper shall come on to be heard on the second day of
the Term, before the Special Paper is gone into.

 2nd. *It is Ordered*, That if notice of any motion, and a copy of the
affidavit or affidavits, on which it is intended to be grounded, shall be
served on the opposite party, his Attorney or Agent, as the case may
be, fourteen days before the Term at which the motion is intended to
be made, a rule absolute may be made in the first instance, if the
Court shall see fit, and in all such cases the cause shall be entered on
the Motion Paper.

Michaelmas Term, 30 Victoria, 1866.

80—*It is Ordered*, That hereafter causes for argument may be entered
on the respective papers on the Monday preceding each Term, and
shall not be entered after the opening of the Court, without leave
given therefor.

 The causes entered on the Motion Paper, shall come on to be heard
immediately after the conclusion of the Common Motions at the beginning of each Term; and the causes upon the other papers respectively shall be taken up in their order, as now provided, immediately
after the Motion Paper is concluded.

Hilary Term, 39 Victoria, 1876.

81—*It is Ordered*, That so much of the Rule of Michaelmas Term,
30th Victoria, as provides that causes entered on the Motion Paper
shall come on to be heard immediately after the conclusion of the
Common Motions at the beginning of each Term, is hereby rescinded;
and that hereafter causes and matters on the Motion Paper shall come
on to be heard on the second day of each Term, as provided by the
Rule of Hillary Term, 6 Wm. IV.

 Notices of motion in Equity. See No. 156.

NEW TRIALS.

Michaelmas Term, 5 William IV, 1834.

82—*It is Ordered*, That in future, the Attorney for the party intending to move for a new trial, or for setting aside a verdict, shall cause to be delivered to the Judge before whom the cause was tried, a note in writing specifying the name of the cause, the time and place of the trial, and the general grounds of the intended motion; such note in writing to be delivered to the Judge in causes tried in vacation, on or before the first day of the next ensuing Term.

Michaelmas Term, 6 William IV, 1835.

83—*It is Ordered*, That no motion for a new trial shall be made after the first Saturday in any Term.

Michaelmas Term, 1 Victoria, 1837.

84—*Whereas* it is desirable, that arguments on rules for new trials or the like, made in causes tried at the Sittings for the County of York, should be heard and disposed of more speedily than can be done under the present practice of the Court; *It is Ordered*, That in future any party intending, after trial had at the said Sittings, to move the Court for a rule to shew cause why a new trial should not be granted, or for any rule of a like description, do give notice to the opposite party of such his intention, together with a note in writing, specifying the general grounds of the intended motion, thirty days before the ensuing term, and that rules *nisi* granted on such motions be made returnable in the same term, unless the Court should see fit, with the consent of parties, or for other good reason, to extend the time for shewing cause to the ensuing term.

Hilary Term 30 Victoria, 1867.

85—*Ordered*, That in future the notices of motions for new trials, or to set aside verdicts, required to be given by the Rules of Michaelmas Term, 5 Wm. IV, and Michaelmas Term, ᵥ Victoria, shall state particularly the grounds of the intended motion.

For example : If the motion is to be made on the grounds of misdirection, or the improper admission or rejection of evidence, the notice shall set forth the particular part or parts of the Judge's direction objected to, and the particular portion or portions of evidence alleged to have been improperly admitted or rejected ; and in like manner on all other grounds, specifying the same separately and distinctly, and as particularly as the circumstances of the case will admit of, and the party shall on the motion be confined to the grounds so specified.

NEW TRIAL FOR YORK SITTINGS.

Easter Term, 18 Victoria, 1855.

86—*It is Ordered,* That when a Rule *nisi* for a new trial—or of the like kind—has been granted in a cause tried at the Sittings for the County of York, the case shall be entered by the Clerk on the special paper for the Term at which the Rule is granted, without its being necessary to serve the Rule *nisi* as in other cases, unless the Court shall order the same to be served; and the cause shall be called on for argument in the order in which it is entered.

Hilary Term, 23 Victoria, 1860.

87—*It is Ordered,* That the Rule of Court of Michaelmas Term, 1st Victoria No. 10, relating to motions for new trials in causes tried at the Sittings for the County of York, shall not apply to causes tried at the Sittings holden in January in each year, but that motions for new trials in causes tried at the said last mentioned Sittings, shall be made as in causes tried at any of the Circuit Courts.

NISI PRIUS RECORD.

See Trials at Nisi Prius.

NISI PRIUS SITTINGS.

Michaelmas Term, 6 William IV, 1835.

88—1st. *It is Ordered,* That there shall be Sittings of Nisi Prius for the County of York, after the respective terms of this Court, on the following days in each and every year, that is to say: Sittings after Hilary Term, on the third Tuesday in February; Sittings after Trinity Term, on the fourth Tuesday in June; Sittings after Michaelmas Term, on the fourth Tuesday in October. The said respective Sittings to continue for so long a time, as in the opinion of the Judge holding the same, may be necessary for the dispatch of the business depending.

2nd. *Ordered,* That the Sheriff of the County of York do summon and return Grand Jurors and Petit Jurors, to attend at the several Sittings in that County, now appointed or hereafter to be appointed, in like manner as has been heretofore accustomed with regard to the terms of this Court; and that hereafter no Jurors be summoned to attend at the Terms, without special order.

3rd *It is Ordered,* That all general rules of this Court, which relate to the entering of causes, the filing of Nisi Prius Records, or other proceedings at Nisi Prius, shall apply to, and be in force at, the Nisi Prius Sittings in the County of York.

4th. *It is Ordered,* That in all actions, in which the issue is made up and the *Venire Facias Juratores* is awarded, as of the last return day, that is to say, the second Satnrday after the first Tuesday, in any term, such Writ of *Venire Facias Juratores* may be awarded, and made returnable forthwith.

Michaelmas Term, 11 Victoria, 1847.

89—*It is Ordered*, That after the present year there shall be Sittings of Nisi Prius for the County of York after the Hilary and Trinity Terms of this Court only, that is to say: Sittings after Hilary Term on the third Tuesday in February in each and every year; and Sittings after Trinity Term on the fourth Tuesday in June in each and every year; the said respective Sittings to continue for so long a time, as in the opinion of the Judge holding the same, may be necessary for the dispatch of the business depending; *And it is further Ordered*, That all the parts of the General Rule of Michaelmas Term in the sixth year of the Reign of King William the Fourth, which relate to Nisi Prius Sittings for the County of York, shall remain in force, excepting the appointment of such Sittings after the Michaelmas Term of this Court.

NON PROS.

See Nos. 42, 43.

NOTICE OF COUNTERMAND.

Hilary Term, 9 George IV, 1828.

90—*It is Ordered*, That no notice of countermand shall be deemed sufficient to save the costs for not proceeding to trial pursuant to notice, unless it be given at least ten days before the time of the intended trial.

Michaelmas Term, 12 Victoria, 1848.

91—*It is Ordered*, That no notice of countermand shall be deemed sufficient to save costs, if any there be, for not proceeding to the execution of a Writ of Inquiry of damages pursuant to notice, unless it be given at least ten days before the time appointed for such Inquiry.

NOTICE OF GROUNDS OF DEFENCE—COPY TO BE FILED WITH NISI PRIUS RECORD.

Trinity Term, 13 Victoria, 1850.

92—*It is Ordered*, That a copy of the notice of any matter of defence delivered with the plea, pursuant to the Act 13th Victoria, cap. 32, and a copy of any order of the Court, or a Judge, which shall have been made touching such notice, shall be filed with the Nisi Prius record at the Court of Nisi Prius, and be annexed to such record.

See Rules Nos. 142, 143.

NOTICE OF GROUNDS FOR NEW TRIAL, ETC.

See New Trial No. 85.

NOTICE OF DEFENCE—NUMBERING GROUNDS— OBJECTIONS—WHEN TAKEN.

Easter Term, 22 Victoria, 1859.

93—*It is Ordered*, That when a notice delivered under the Act of Assembly, 13th Victoria, cap. 32, includes several distinct grounds of defence, which would, before such Act, have required separate pleas, such separate grounds of defence be numbered consecutively and placed in several clauses; but any objection to the form of the notice, on the ground of duplicity, must be made to a Judge within fourteen days after the same is delivered, who will upon summons, make such order for allowance or disallowance of the notice, or amendment of the same, and on such terms as the case may require; and no objection to the notice on the ground of duplicity will be allowed at the trial of the cause.

NOTICE OF TRIAL AND INQUIRY.

Hilary Term, 9 George IV, 1828.

94—*It is Ordered*, That from henceforth there be *at least* fourteen days' notice of trial, and for Writs of Inquiry, in all cases, whether the defendant lives within the County where the Court sits or not; any former rule of this Court to the contrary notwithstanding.

NOTICE OF GROUNDS FOR NEW TRIAL.
See No. 85.

NOTICE OF JUDGMENT AS IN CASE OF NON-SUIT.
See Judgment as in Case of Non-suit.

OATH OF CONSTABLE—RETIRING OF JURY,

Easter Term, 18 Victoria, 1855.

95—The oath of the Constable, who shall have charge of the Jury, shall be as follows:

You shall keep this Jury together in one of the Jury Rooms of this Court House [*or as the place may be*] until their verdict is agreed on, or the Court shall otherwise order; you shall not suffer any person to speak to them, or any of them, neither shall you yourself speak to them, unless it be to ask if they are agreed on their verdict, except by direction of the Court.—So help your God.

PAPERS ANNEXED TO AFFIDAVITS (MARKING OFF.
See Nos. 3, 4.

PAPERS TAKEN OFF THE FILES OF COURT.

Hilary Term, 31 Victoria, 1868.

96—1st. *Ordered,* That all papers which may have been taken off the files of this Court, either on the Equity or Common Law side, under the order of the Court or any Judge thereof, by any Attorney or other person, be forthwith returned to the Clerk of this Court and restored to their respective files.

2nd. No record, paper or document on file in the Office of the Clerk of this Court shall hereafter be removed therefrom, except under the especial order of the Court or one of the Judges thereof, to be obtained only on it being made clearly to appear by affidavit to the Court or Judge, that the original record, paper or document is indispensably necessary to be used in some Court of this Province, or before a Judge thereof, and that a copy of such record, paper or document cannot be used in lieu thereof.

3rd. The Clerk of the Pleas or the Clerk in Equity, as the case may be, shall enter in a Book the title of the cause, the descriptions of the record or papers, the date of removal, and the name of the Attorney on whose application any such order shall have been granted; and shall enclose the record or papers permitted to be removed, in a sealed envelope, indorsing thereon a description of the record or papers enclosed, and direct the same to the Clerk of the Circuits or the Clerk of the Court in which the same are to be used to be delivered to the presiding Judge at the Circuit or Court where it is intended to use them, and shall himself place the same in the possession of the said Clerk, or remit the same to him by Mail if necessary; and if such records or papers are required to be used on the trial, the presiding Judge shall break the seal of the envelope, and deliver the said records or papers to the custody of the Clerk of the Court during the progress of the trial, and such Clerk shall, at the conclusion of the trial, again enclose and seal up the said records or papers, and after being identified by the signature or initials of the presiding Judge, shall forthwith return the same to the proper custodian.

PARCHMENT—PATENT (USE OF PROHIBITED).

Hilary Term, 25 Victoria, 1862.

97—*It is Ordered,* That from and after the first day of Easter Term next, the article called and known as *patent parchment*, be not used for the Writs and Records of this Court.

PERSONS OTHER THAN ATTORNEYS CONDUCTING SUITS—FEES ON FILING PAPERS.

Easter Term, 12 Victoria, 1849.

98—*It is Ordered,* That where parties who are not Attorneys of this Court, prosecute or defend any action in person, no papers, writs or records
5

be received or filed in the Clerk's Office, or entries made, without the fees being paid thereon at the time of such filing or entering.

PAYMENT OF MONEY INTO COURT.

Trinity Term, 2 Victoria, 1889.

99—1st. *Whereas* by an Act passed in the first year of Her Majesty's reign, intituled " An Act for the further amendment of the Law," it is enacted "that it shall and may be lawful for the defendant in all personal actions pending or to be brought in the Supreme Court of this Province, (except actions for assault and battery, false imprisonment, libel, slander, malicious arrest or prosecution, criminal conversation or debauching of the plaintiff's daughter or servant,) by leave of the said Court or a Judge of such Court, to pay into the said Court a sum of money by way of compensation or amends, in such manner and under such regulations as to the payment of costs, and the form of pleading, as the said Court, or any three of the Judges thereof, shall, by any rules or orders by them to be from time to time made, order and direct."

2nd. *Ordered,* That when money is paid into Court under the said Act, such payment shall be pleaded, and as near as may be in the following form, *mutatis mutandis :—*

" C. D. ⎫ And the said defendant comes by E. F., his Attorney," 3rd. ats. * ⎬ (*or* " in person, etc.") and says (*or in case it be pleaded as* A. B. ⎭ *to part only, add* " as to —— being part of the sum in the Declaration, or —— Count of the Declaration mentioned," *or* as to the residue of the sum of ——) that the plaintiff ought not further to maintain his action, because the defendant now brings into Court the sum of —— ready to be paid to the plaintiff, and the defendant further says that the plaintiff has not sustained damages (*or in actions of debt* "that he is not indebted to the plaintiff") to a greater amount than the said sum of etc., in respect to the cause of action in the Declaration mentioned," (*or* " in the introductory part of the plea mentioned) and this he, the defendant, is ready to verify, wherefore he prays judgment, if the plaintiff ought further to maintain his action thereof against him ;" and no other plea shall be pleaded to the said action, or to so much thereof as the said plea of payment into Court is applicable.

4th. *It is Ordered,* That upon a rule or Judge's order being made for paying money into Court under the said Act, the money shall be paid to the Clerk at the time of filing the plea, together with his poundage thereon, and the Clerk shall make a minute of such payment in the margin of the plea, and shall also give a memorandum of such payment to be delivered with the copy of the plea to the plaintiff's Attorney ; which sum shall be paid out to the plaintiff's Attorney on demand.

5th. *It is Ordered,* That the plaintiff, after delivery of a plea of payment of money into Court, shall be at liberty to reply to the same, by accepting the sum so paid into Court in full satisfaction and discharge of the cause of action, in respect of which it has been paid in, and he shall be at liberty in that case to tax his costs of suit, and in case of non-payment thereof within ten days, to sign judgment for his costs of suit; or the plaintiff may reply " that he has sustained damages" (*or* " that the defendant was and is indebted to him" *as the case may be*) to a greater amount than the said sum ; and in the event of an issue thereon being found for the defendant, the defendant shall be entitled to judgment and his cost of suit : Provided that if the sum of money paid into Court in any action not summary would have been recoverable under the summary form, the plaintiff, if he take the money out of Court in discharge of the action, shall not be entitled to more than summary costs, unless he obtain the order of the Court or a Judge for the larger costs, upon good cause shewn therefor.

PLEA (ABATEMENT.)

See No. 1.

PLEAS (DELIVERY OF.)

Hilary Term, 6 Victoria, 1843.

100—*Ordered*, That in future copies of all pleas shall be delivered to the plaintiff's Attorney within the time allowed for pleading ; otherwise the plaintiff shall be at liberty (demand of plea being duly made) to sign interlocutory judgment : and that it shall not be necessary to search for a plea before such signing, after the expiration of the rule to plead.

PLEAS (DEMAND OF.)

Trinity Term, 5 Victoria, 1842.

101—*Ordered*, That where the Attorneys for the respective parties reside in different counties, the defendant's Attorney shall be allowed seven days after demand of plea, wherein to file the plea, and serve the opposite Attorney with a copy thereof, unless the demand be accompanied by a direction to deliver a copy of the plea to some person resident in the same place in which the defendant's Attorney resides ; in which case such copy of plea must be delivered within twenty-four hours, according to the present practice, and the plea forthwith transmitted to the Clerk for filing.

PRACTICE IN EQUITY—SERVICE ON NON-RESIDENTS.

Trinity Term, 19 Victoria, 1856.

102—1st. Upon any suit being commenced against any defendant, if it shall be made to appear upon affidavit that such defendant doth not reside within the Province, but has a known place of residence without the limits thereof, an order may be made for the appearance of such defendant at a certain day therein named, and a copy of such order shall within one year be served upon such defendant either personally or by delivering the same at the residence of said defendant to some adult person belonging to his family; and if such defendant do not appear within the time limited by such order or such further time as the Court may appoint, the plaintiff shall be entitled to the like decree, as in case of non-appearance, when the defendant is served with process within the Province—provided, that in case the defendant reside in any part of Europe or the West Indies, such service be made three calendar months before the day of appearance, and if such defendant reside in any part of the United States of America or in any of the British North American Colonies, such service shall be made two calendar months before the day of appearance; and if in any other part of the world, such service shall be made six calendar months before the day of appearance.

2nd. The proof of such service may be made by affidavit sworn before any Judge of any Superior Court in the Country where the same is made, or the Mayor or other Chief Magistrate of any City, Borough or Town corporate in any part of Her Majesty's Dominions —provided always, that where the same is sworn in any Country, not part of Her Majesty's Dominions, it shall be authenticated by a certificate under the hand and seal of the British Ambassador, Envoy, Minister, Consul or Vice-Consul; and if in any part of the British Dominions, by a certificate under the hand and seal of a Public Notary.

3rd. The provisions contained in the fourteenth section of the second chapter of the Act relating to the administration of justice in Equity are hereby rescinded.

4th. The order for hearing the cause in the manner provided for by the fifteenth section of the last named chapter of the said Act, instead of the time therein appointed, may be made within one calendar month after the cause shall be at issue, on service of notice and of a copy of the affidavit on which the application is to be made, on the opposite party, ten days before such application, the time for hearing which shall have been previously appointed by the Judge to whom the same is to be made; provided, that in cases which are already at issue, the order may be made within one calendar month from the Saturday next after the second Tuesday in the present term.

PRISONERS—PROCEEDINGS AGAINST.

Hilary Term, 2 Victoria, 1839.

103—1st. *It is Ordered,* That from and after the last day of this term, in all cases where a prisoner is or shall be taken, detained or charged in custody by mesne process thereafter returnable, issuing out of this Court, and the plaintiff shall not cause a declaration against such prisoner to be delivered to such prisoner, or to the Sheriff in whose custody such prisoner is or shall be detained or charged, within three calendar months after the return of the process by virtue whereof such prisoner is or shall be taken, detained, or charged in custody; and cause an affidavit to be made and filed with the Clerk of this Court, of the delivery of such declaration, and of the time when, and the person to whom the same was delivered, before the last day of the term next after the, delivery of such declaration, the prisoner shall be discharged out of custody by writ of *supersedeas* to be granted by this Court, or one of the Judges thereof, úpon filing common bail; unless upon notice given to the plaintiff's Attorney, good cause shall be shewn to the contrary; and in case of a commitment or render in discharge of bail, after the return of process, and before a declaration delivered, unless the plaintiff's shall cause a declaration to be delivered, and an affidavit thereof made and filed; before the end of the term next after such commitment or render shall be made, and due notice of such render given, the prisoner shall be discharged out of custody by writ of *supersedeas* to be granted as aforesaid, upon filing common bail, unless upon notice given to the plaintiff's Attorney good cause shall be shewn to the contrary.

2nd. That on every declaration so to be delivered against a prisoner as aforesaid, a rule to appear and plead shall be indorsed according to the form following, that is to say, "The defendant, C. D., is to appear and plead hereto at the suit of the plaintiff, A. B., within twenty days after service of this declaration; otherwise judgment will be entered against him by default."

G. H., Plaintiff's Attorney.

————— 18

And that judgment shall not be entered against such defendant by default until the expiration of the said rule.

3rd. That the Sheriff, who shall have received a copy of a declaration against any prisoner in his custody, shall indorse thereon the time of his so receiving the same, and shall forthwith deliver the same to the said prisoner, and shall also enter in a book to be by him kept for. that purpose, the time of receiving such declaration, and of delivering the same to the prisoner.

4th. That where the plaintiff declares against the prisoner, it shall not be necessary to make more than two copies of the declaration, of which one shall be served, and the other filed with an affidavit of service, and a copy of the Rule to appear and plead indorsed thereon.

5th. That upon application made by the plaintiff, before the time at which the defendant may be supersedable, and good and sufficient cause shewn by affidavit, further time to declare may be given by rule of Court or order of a Judge.

6th. That upon every application for a *supersedeas* for want of declaring in due time, in addition to the certificate of the Sheriff that no declaration has been delivered to him for the prisoner, there shall be an affidavit of the defendant, that he has not been served with such declaration.

7th. That unless the plaintiff shall proceed to trial or final judgment within three terms next after the delivery or filing of declaration, if by the course of this Court the plaintiff can so proceed; of which three terms, the term wherein such declaration shall be delivered shall be taken to be one; or, if by the course of the Court the plaintiff cannot so proceed to trial or final judgment within the time above limited; then unless the plaintiff shall proceed to trial or final judgment as soon after as by the course of this Court he may so proceed, the prisoner shall be discharged out of custody by writ of *supersedeas* to be granted as aforesaid, upon filing common bail, unless upon notice given to the plaintiff's Attorney, good cause shall be shewn to the contrary.

8th. That in all cases after final judgment obtained against a prisoner, unless the plaintiff shall cause such prisoner to be charged in execution, within three calendar months next after the day on which such final judgment shall be signed—in case no writ of error shall be depending, nor injunction be obtained for stay of proceedings; and if any writ of error shall be depending or injunction be obtained, then within three calendar months next after judgment shall be affirmed, the writ of error be non-prossed or discontinued, or the injunction dissolved; the prisoner shall be discharged out of custody by *supersedeas* to be granted as aforesaid, unless upon notice given to the plaintiff's Attorney, good cause shall be shewn to the contrary.

9th. That after trial had, unless the plaintiff do proceed to have his judgment entered up and signed as soon as by the course and practice of this Court he may so do, or within one calendar month thereafter, in case no such injunction shall be obtained or order made for stay of proceedings; and if any such injunction shall be obtained, or order made, then within one calendar month after such injunction shall be dissolved or order discharged the prisoner shall be discharged out of custody, in like manner as in the last preceding rule is provided.

10th. That in case of a render in discharge of bail after final judgment obtained, unless the plaintiff shall cause the defendant to be charged in execution within three calendar months next after such render and due notice thereof given; and in case of render after trial and before judgment, unless the plaintiff do proceed to have his judgment entered up and signed within the time limited by the last preceding rule, or within one calendar month after such render and due notice thereof, the prisoner shall be entitled to his discharge in manner aforesaid, unless good cause be shewn to the contrary.

11th. That no treaty or agreement shall be sufficient cause to prevent any prisoner's having the benefit of a *supersedeas*, unless the same be in writing, signed by the prisoner or his Attorney, or some person duly authorized by such prisoner.

RECOGNIZANCE ROLL.

Easter Term, 11 Victoria, 1848.

104—No Recognizance Roll or a Recognizance of Bail to be received or filed until it is ascertained, upon search, that the Recognizance or Bail-piece is on file.

RECORDS—WRITS—DOCKETS—JUDGMENT ROLLS.

Easter Term, 25 George III, 1785.

105—1st. *It is Ordered*, That all the Processes, Records, Rolls, and Judgments of this Court, be made on parchment, according to the usage of the Court of King's Bench in England.

2nd. That the Bill issued out of the Court of King's Bench in England, commonly called the Bill of Middlesex, be the first process *ad Respondendum*, where it is to be executed by the Sheriff of the County where the Court sits; and that the first process, going into other Counties, shall be a common *Capias*, in form of the *alias* or *Latitat*, leaving out the words "as before we have commanded you," except where it is actually the *Alias Capias;* the recital of the issuing and returning a Bill being now supposed unnecessary.

3rd. That every Attorney of this Court enter the return, and file the Writ or Process, in all actions which have not been agreed, and in which they intend to proceed; and shall make a docket of all such returns and rules, and on the last day of the term shall deliver the same to the Clerk of the Court; and shall pay to the Clerk his own fees, as well as those of the Judges and Crier, in such actions.

Hilary Term, 45 George III, 1805.

106—*It is Ordered*, That the Clerk of this Court be in future authorized to deliver blank Writs, signed and sealed, to the several and respective Attorneys of this Court, to be by them filled up as occasion may require ; they accounting to the said Clerk therefor, and forthwith forwarding to him proper Præcipes for such of the said Writs as they may from time to time fill up and issue, in the same manner as is practiced by the Filacers in England.

Hilary Term, 50 George III, 1810.

107—1st. *It is Ordered*, That the Rolls of all Judgments entered at the several Terms be brought in and filed on or before the first day of the Term next after the Term in which they shall be respectively entered.

2nd. That in all cases where blank Writs shall be filled up by the Attorneys, the Præcipes and Affidavits for Bail, in cases of Bailable process, be transmitted to the Clerk's Office by the very first opportunity, after issuing the Process; and that no Attorney do, on any account, suffer any blank Writ to go out of his hands to be filled up and issued by any other than an Attorney of this Court —and that no Rule to plead or other proceeding in the cause be had, unless the Præcipe and the Affidavit, in cases where an Affidavit is made, be duly filed.

3rd. That all Judgment Rolls be engrossed upon Parchment in a fair legible hand, with a margin of not less than an inch in breath, and a sufficient space at the top for binding up the same, and at the bottom for numbering the Roll; and that no Roll be received or filed by the Clerk that is not made up in the mann·r herein directed.

4th. That no Processes be signed or filed by the Clerk which are not engrossed upon Parchment agreeably to the former Rule of this Court in that behalf made.

5th. That the Rule respecting the filing of Dockets and payment of Fees be stri.tly enforced, and that the Clerk report to the Court any delinquency in this respect without delay.

Hilary Term, 60 George III, 1820.

108—*Whereas*, by a standing Rule of this Court, made and entered of Easter Term, in the twenty-fifth year of His Majesty s reign; *It is Ordered*, "That every Attorney of this Court enter the return and file the Writs or Process in all actions which have not been agreed, and in which they intend to proceed, and shall make a Docket of all such Returns and Rules, and on the last day of the Term shall deliver the same, with the Writs and Processes in such actions to the Clerk of the Court, and shall pay to the Clerk of the Court his own fees, as well as those of the Judges and Crier in such actions;" *and whereas*, notwithstanding the repeated orders of this Court, enjoining a strict and punctual compliance with the said Rule, the same has been in various instances violated and neglected: *It is hereby Ordered*, That in future, if any Attorney of this Court shall neglect a compliance with the said Rule, in every respect, agreeable to the true intent and meaning thereof. on or before the first day of the Term next after the Term in which such Rule ought to have been complied with, every such Attorney shall be considered as in contempt of the Court, on account of such neglect of, and disobedience to the said Rule. And the Clerk of this Court is hereby enjoined not to receive or file from, or for, any such Attorney, at any time afterwards, any Writ, Præcipe, Process, or any other paper or proceedings whatever, of a date subsequent to the Term in which such Rule ought to have been complied with, until such contempt shall have been purged by a compliance with the said Rule. And the Clerk is further enjoined, on the second day of the Term next after the Term in which the said Rule ought to have been complied with, to prepare, and deliver to the Court, the name or names of all such Attorneys as shall be so in contempt as aforesaid.

Michaelmas Term, 6 George IV, 1825.

109—1st. Upon reference to the Rule of Hilary Term, 45 George III, relating to the delivery of blank Writs to the Attorneys of this Court.

2nd. *It is Ordered,* That from and after Hilary Term next, no Attorney of this Court do presume to issue any Writ or Process whatever, unless the same be actually signed and sealed by the proper Officer of this Court; and that the Clerk of the Pleas do forthwith furnish a copy of this Rule to every Attorney of this Court.

Hilary Term, 7 William IV, 1837.

110—*It is Ordered,* That from and after this present Hilary Term, every Attorney of this Court enter the return and file the Writ or Process in all actions which have not at or before such return been settled or discontinued, and make and file with the Clerk a docket of all such returns and rules, on or before the last return day of the term at which such Writs are returnable, or within thirty days thereafter; and that the Clerk do not in future receive or file any docket, or enter any such rule after the said thirty days, without the special order of the Court or a Judge, to be made on affidavit or affidavits, properly accounting for the delay.

Trinity Term, 23 Victoria, 1860.

111—*It is Ordered,* That the following Regulations be observed in the Office of the Clerk of the Crown in this Court:

Blank Writs issued by Clerk.

1st. Blank Writs of Habeas Corpus, and any others which require the fiat of a Judge to be endorsed thereon before they can be issued for the purpose of being executed, and Blank Writs of Subpœna may be delivered to the respective Attorneys of this Court signed and sealed, to be by them filled up as occasion may require; they accounting to the Clerk therefor, and forwarding to his office proper Præcipes for such of the said Writs as they may from time to time fill up and issue, stating in the Præcipes the name of the Judge whose fiat has been indorsed, where a fiat is necessary.

2nd. No other Blank Writs than those above specified, to be signed and sealed; nor shall any mere blank pieces of parchment be signed and sealed by the Clerk of the Crown.

REPLEVIN.
Easter Term, 50 George III, 1810.

112—*It is Ordered,* That the Writ of Replevin, under the Act of Assembly 50 George III, c. 21, be in the form following, viz.:

"George the Third, by the Grace of God, of the United Kingdom
(L. s.)   of Great Britain and Ireland, King, Defender of the Faith, etc.,
etc., etc.

To the Sheriff of   GREETING.

"We command you if A. B. shall make you secure of prosecuting his complaint, and also of returning the Goods and Chattels, to wit: which C. D. hath taken and unjustly detained

6

as it is alleged, if a return thereof shall be adjudged, that then the Goods and Chattels aforesaid, to him, the said A. B. without delay you cause to be replevied and delivered ; aud put by sureties and safe pledges, the aforesaid C. D., that he be before us at Fredericton on the   Tuesday in   next, to answer to the said A. B. of a Plea, wherefore he took the said Goods and Chattels of the said A. B.; and then unjustly detained against gages and pledges, as he saith, and have there then the names of the pledges and this Writ. Witness   at Fredericton, the   day of   in the year of our Reign." And if the defendant shall not appear at the return of such Writ, or within twenty days after the return thereof, then the plaintiff shall be at liberty to issue a Process against such defendant, returnable at the next ensuing Term, in the following form, viz. .

" George the Third, by the Grace of God, of the United Kingdom
(L. S.)   of Great Britain and Ireland, King, Defender of the Faith, etc., etc., etc.

To the Sheriff of   GREETING.

" We command you that you take C. D., if he shall be found in your Bailiwick, and him safely keep, so that you may have his body before us, at Fredericton, on the   Tuesday in   next, to answer A. B. of a Plea, wherefore he took the Goods and Chattels of the said A. B., and them unjustly detained against gages and pledges, as he saith, and have you there then this Writ

Witness   at Fredericton, the   day of   in the   year of our Reign."
And shall serve such defendant personally with a copy of such Process, upon which copy shall be written an English notice to such defendant, of the intent and meaning of such service ; which notice shall be in the form used in the service of Processes in actions in which no affidavit shall be made and filed of the cause of action ; and if such defendant shall not appear at the return of such Process, or within twenty days after such return, the plaintiff shall be at liberty, upon the usual Affidavit being made and filed of the personal service of such Process, to enter a common appearance, or file common bail for such defendant, and to proceed thereon as if such defendant had entered his or her appearance or filed common bail.

And it is further Ordered, That in all cases in which the Sheriff shall be a party, the foregoing Processes shall be directed to the Coroner, as in other cases in which the Sheriff is a party.

Michaelmas Term, 22 Victoria, 1858.

113—*It is Ordered*, That when upon the trial of any action of replevin, the defence arises under the 15th and 16th Sections of Chapter 126 of the Revised Statutes, and upon the plea of *non cepit* a verdict is found for the defendant, the *postea* be in the form following, with such variations as the case may require :

" Afterwards, etc., [*in the usual form*] say upon their oaths, that the said defendant did take and detain the said goods and chattels mentioned in the said declaration, as a distress for rent upon certain premises enjoyed by the said plaintiff under a grant or demise at a certain rent, and that there was due to the defendant for such rent at the time of making the distress, and still is due the sum of——, and they assess the damages of the said defendant by reason of the premises for the said rent, and the costs and charges of making the said distress, at the sum of ——, pursuant to Chapter 126 of the Revised Statutes, besides his costs and charges, etc."

If the Bailiff of the landlord, or any one acting in aid of the landlord, be made a defendant, the *postea* may be varied, as follows :

" And that there was due to the defendant, C. D., etc., [*as before*] and that the said defendant, E. F., was, at the time of making the said distress, the Bailiff of the said C. D.," *or* "that the said E. F. was then and there present, aiding and assisting the said C. D. in making the said distress, etc."

And that the entry of judgment on the said *postea* be in the form following, with the requisite variations as before, according to the circumstances of the case :

" Therefore it is considered that the said plaintiff take nothing by his suit, but that the said defendant do go thereof without day, etc. ; and it is further considered, that the said defendant (*or* that the said defendant C. D.) do recover against the said plaintiff the said sum of ——, for his damages so assessed as aforesaid, and also —— for his costs and charges, by the Court of our said Lady the Queen now here adjudged to the said defendant, according to the said Revised Statutes; which said damages, costs and charges in the whole amount to ——, and that the said defendant have execution thereof."

NOTE.—See form of Writ, 1 Rev. Stat., Title xxxiv. cap. 126.

REPLEVIN BONDS.

Michaelmas Term, 4 Victoria, 1840.

See 1 Revised Statutes, cap. 126.

114—*Whereas*, the Justices of the Supreme Court, or any three of them, are authorized and required by the Act of Assembly 3 Victoria, c. 63, intituled, " An Act further to regulate proceedings in Replevin by allowing damages in certain cases to the defendant," to frame and prescribe suitable and proper forms for the Replevin Bonds hereafter to be taken, and for the entering of any verdict or judgment pursuant to the said Act, such forms from the time of the said Act taking effect, to be observed and complied with in the same manner as if the same were in the Act specified and contained, and such forms to be applicable to the Inferior Court of Common Pleas as well as the Supreme Court. Provided that nothing in the said Act contained, shall extend or be construed to extend to affect any proceedings in any action of Replevin commenced before the said Act goes into operation : *It is*

Ordered, That upon and after the first day of January, 1841, being the time appointed for the said Act to commence and take effect, the following forms framed pursuant to the said Act shall be used, with such alterations as the description of the Court, the Officer to whom the Writ is directed, the number and character of the parties or the circumstances of the case may render necessary; but that any variance not being matter of substance shall not affect the validity of the Bonds or entries.

NO. I.—REPLEVIN BONDS.

KNOW ALL MEN BY THESE PRESENTS, That we (name and additions of plaintiff and his sureties) are jointly and severally held and firmly bound unto   Esquire, Sheriff of the County of   (or City and County as the case may be) in the sum of   (double the value of the goods to be replevied) of lawful money of New Brunswick, to be paid to the said   , his certain Attorney, Executors, Administrators or Assigns; for which payment to be well and truly made, we bind ourselves and each of us, our and each and every of our Heirs, Executors and Administrators, firmly by these Presents, sealed with our Seals.

Dated the   day of   in the   year of the Reign of our Sovereign Lady Victoria, by the Grace of God of the United Kingdom of Great Britain and Ireland, Queen, Defender of the Faith, etc., and in the year of our Lord one thousand eight hundred and

The Condition of this Obligation is such, That if the above bounden (plaintiff) do appear before our said Lady the Queen, at Fredericton, on (the return day of the Writ of Replevin) and do then and there prosecute his suit with effect and without delay against (the defendant) for taking and unjustly detaining his goods and chattels, to wit; (here specify the goods to be replevied) and do make a return of the said goods and chattels, if a return of the same shall be adjudged, and do pay all such damages as may be awarded to the said (defendant) pursuant to the Act of Assembly, made and passed in the third year of Her Majesty's reign, intituled "An Act further to regulate proceedings in Replevin," by allowing damages in certain cases to the defendant; then this Obligation to be void, otherwise to remain in full force and virtue.

Sealed and delivered in \
   the presence of   }

IF THE WRIT BE ISSUED OUT OF ANY INFERIOR COURT OF COMMON PLEAS, THE CONDITION OF THE BOND WILL BE AS FOLLOWS:

"The condition of this Obligation is such, that if the above bounden (the plaintiff) do appear before the Justices of the Inferior Court of Common Pleas for the said County of   at   on   (as specified in the Writ, *or* before the Recorder of the said City of Saint John at the next Inferior Court of Common Pleas, to be holden for the said City and County at the said City on, etc.,) then (conclude as in the foregoing form.)

NO. 2.—VERDICT ON POSTEA WHERE DAMAGES ARE AWARDED TO THE
DEFENDANT.

(Commence in the usual form). Say upon their oaths, that (stating
the negative or affirmative of the pleading which concludes to the
Country, according as it makes for the defendant) in manner and form
as the said   hath "complained against him" *or* "in pleading
alleged," and they assess the damages of the said defendant by reason
of the premises to   pursuant to the Act of Assembly in such
case made and provided, besides his costs and charges, etc., (as in the
usual form.)

No. 3.—ENTRY OF JUDGMENT ON THE ABOVE.

Therefore it is considered, that the said plaintiff take nothing
by his suit, but that the said defendant do go thereof without day,
etc., and that he have a return of the said goods and chattels, to hold
to him irreplevisable for ever. And it is further considered, that the
said defendant do recover against the said plaintiff his said damages,
costs and charges, by the jurors aforesaid in form aforesaid assessed,
and also   for his said costs and charges by the Court of our
said Lady the Queen, now here (or in the Inferior Court " by the
Justices here") adjudged of increase to the defendant, according to
the form of the Statute in such case made and provided ; which said
damages, costs and charges, in the whole amount to   , and that
the said defendant have execution thereof.

No. 4.—ENTRY OF VERDICT ON POSTEA WHERE THE VALUE OF THE GOODS IS ASSESSED BY THE JURY.

(*Commence as in form No. 2.*) In manner and form as the said
hath complained against him, (or in pleading alleged,) and at the
prayer of the said defendant they further say upon their oaths aforesaid, that the said goods and chattels at the time of the replevying
thereof, were worth   according to the true value thereof, which
they award to the said defendant in damages according to the form of
the Act of Assembly in such case made and provided ; and they assess
the defendant's other damages by reason of the premises to
pursuant to the said Act, besides his costs and charges, etc., (as in the
usual form.)

No. 5.—ENTRY OF JUDGMENT ON THE ABOVE.

Therefore it is considered, that the said plaintiff take nothing by his
suit, but that the said defendant do go thereof without day, etc. And
it is further considered, that the said defendant do recover against the
said plaintiff the said sum of   being the value of the goods and
chattels aforesaid by the Jury in form aforesaid assessed : and also
for his said other damages, costs and charges, by the Court of
our said Lady the Queen, now here, (or in the Inferior Court " by the
Justices here,") adjudged of increase to the said defendant, according
to the form of the Statute in such case made and provided ; which
said damages, costs and charges, in the whole amount to
and that the said defendant have execution thereof.

RULE (CONSENT.)

Trinity Term, 7 George IV, 1826.

115—*Whereas* by the common Consent Rule in actions of ejectment, the defendant is required to confess Lease, Entry, and Ouster, and insist upon his title only; and whereas in many instances of late years, defendants in ejectment, have put the plaintiff, after the title of the Lessor of the plaintiff has been established, to give evidence that such defendant was in possession, at the time the ejectment was brought, of the premises mentioned in the ejectment, and for want of such proof, have caused such plaintiffs to be non-suited;

> *And whereas* such practice is contrary to the true intent and meaning of such Consent Rule, and of the provisions therein contained, for the defendant's insisting upon the title only: *It is therefore Ordered*, That from henceforth in every action of ejectment, the defendant shall specify in the Consent Rule for what premises he intends to defend, and shall consent in such Rule, to confess upon the trial, that the defendant (if he defends as Tenant, or in case he defends as Landlord, that his Tenant) was, at the time of the service of the declaration, in the possession of such premises; and that if upon the trial the defendant shall not confess such possession, as well as Lease, Entry, and Ouster, whereby the plaintiff shall not be able further to prosecute his suit against the said defendant, then no costs shall be allowed for not further prosecuting the same, but the said defendant shall pay costs to the plaintiff in that case to be taxed.

Trinity Term, 8 Victoria, 1845.

116—*Ordered*, That in every action of ejectment, when any person or persons shall apply to be made defendant or defendants in such action, and be allowed to enter into a special consent rule to admit Lease and Entry, but not Ouster, unless an actual Ouster of the lessor of the plaintiff by him or them should be proved, on the ground that the defence to the action will involve a question of joint tenancy or tenancy in common; the affidavit on which such application is founded shall state the person or persons with whom the party so applying, claims to be joint tenant or tenant in common, and that he is advised and believes that he is joint tenant or tenant in common, with such person or persons.

RETURN OF WRIT.

See Side-Bar Rule.

RULES TO PLEAD.

Easter Term, 25 George III, 1785.

117—That all defendants have twenty days to plead from the day of the notice in writing delivered of the filing such Declaration, except where the defendant is returned in custody; in which case the defendant shall have twenty days to plead, from the time of serving a copy of the Declaration, and of the rule to plead, to be served on the Sheriff or defendant.

SCIRE FACIAS.

See Writ of.

SECURITY OF COSTS.

Michaelmas Term, 8 Victoria, 1844.

118—*Ordered*, That the rule of Trinity Term, 30 George III, be rescinded, and that in future where security for costs is ordered, such security shall be given in the sum of forty pounds in all cases, except in summary; and that in summary cases, security shall be given in the sum of twenty pounds.

SERVICE OF NOTICES.

Easter Term, 25 George III, 1785.

119—That all notices to be served on defendants, or the Attorneys of either party, shall be deemed well served if left at the dwelling house, or last, or most usual place of his or their lodgings.

2nd. That all notices be served on the Attorneys for the parties, except notices of exception to Bail, which may be served on the defendant or his Attorney, or on the person who serves the notice of Bail.

Hilary Term, 28 Victoria, 1865.

120—*Ordered*, That no service of any paper on an Attorney in any cause, shall be deemed good service by leaving such paper at his dwelling house or last place of abode, unless it shall appear by the affidavit of service that the Attorney has no Office, or if having an Office, that the same was closed, or if open, that there was no person in such Office upon whom service could be made ; in any of which cases, leaving the same at the dwelling house or last place of residence of the Attorney, shall be deemed sufficient service thereof.

SERVICE OF PROCESS.

Trinity Term, 3 Victoria, 1840.

121—*It is Ordered*, That from and after the first day of Michaelmas term next, when service of Process is affected at' the usual place of abode of the defendant, pursuant to the Act 7 Wm. 4, c, 14. s. 1, the Affidavit of such service shall be in the following form, or to that effect, in order to entitle the Plaintiff to an order for perfecting such service.

Form of Affidavit.

A. B. (name, residence and addition of Deponent) maketh oath and saith, that he, this deponent, did on the   day of   deliver a true copy of the annexed Writ or Process, at the house of C. D., the defendant, named in such Writ or Process, (or the house of any other person as the case may be,) situate in the Parish of   in the County of   , unto E. F., the wife of such defendant, (or to G. H. an adult person residing in the said house, and known to this deponent as a member or inmate of the family of such defendant) and this deponent further saith, that the said house was at the time of such delivery the usual place of abode of such defendant, and that the said copy of the said Process was accompanied with an English notice in writing to the defendant, of the intent and meaning of the service of such Process, pursuant to the Statute in such case made and provided; and this deponent further saith, that at the time of making such service of the said Process, the said defendant was not, as this deponent verily believes, without the limits of the said County.

Easter Term, 13 Victoria, 1850.

122—1st. *Whereas* by the Act of Assembly 12th Victoria, cap. 39, sec. 44, the Act of Assembly 7th William 4, cap 14, allowing service of Process to be made at the usual place of abode of the defendants, is repealed and the said Act of 12th Victoria, limits and restricts service of Process at the dwelling to cases where the defendant shall be within the jurisdiction of the Court, at the time of such service; and the Rule Nó. 2 of this Court of Trinity Term, 3rd Victoria, is thereby virtually superseded : *It is Ordered*, That such Rule be rescinded, and that the affidavit of such service shall be in the following form, or to that effect, in order to entitle the plaintiff to an order for perfecting such service :

"A. B., Sheriff of ———, (or A. B., of ———, a Deputy of the Sheriff of ———,) maketh oath and saith, that he, this deponent, did on the ——— day of ———, deliver a true copy of the annexed writ or process at the house of C. D., the defendant named in such writ or process, (or the house of any other person, as the case may be,) situate in the Parish of ———, in the County of ———, unto E. F., the wife of such defendant, (or to G. H., an adult person residing in the said house, and known to this deponent as a member or inmate of the family of such defendant) ; and this deponent further saith, that the said house was at the time of such delivery the usual place of abode of such defendant, [and that the said copy of the said process was accompanied with an English notice in writing to the defendant, of the intent and meaning of the service of such process, pursuant to the Statute in such case made and provided];* and this deponent further saith, that the said defendant was at the time of such service within the limits of this Province, as this deponent knows, for the following reasons, (here state the particular means of knowledge the deponent has of the defendant's

---

* The clause between brackets may be omitted in the service of Summary Writs.

being within the Province; if this fact is not known to the serving officer it may be proved by the affidavit of another person; and the affidavit of the serving officer may omit the words after * and conclude as follows :—] and this deponent further saith, that he verily believes that at the time of such service the defendant was within this Province."

2nd. *It is further Ordered*, That in order to entitle the plaintiff to an order for making a service at the dwelling good service, the Writ or Process shall be delivered to the Sheriff of the County into which it is issued for service, and that such service be effected, and the affidavit thereof made by the Sheriff, or his general or special Deputy.

3rd. *It is further Ordered*, That these Rules shall apply *mutatis mutandis* to Writs directed to the Coroner.

4th. *It is further Ordered*, That these Rules apply to every Writ or Process issued after the end of the present Term.

Trinity Term, 20 Victoria, 1857.

Service of Process on Non-Residents.

123—*It is Ordered*, That where service of process is made on persons resident out of the Province, under the Act of Assembly 14 Victoria, cap. 2, the nature and place of the business carried on by the defendant in the Province, and the particular nature of the agency or employment of the person with whom the copy of Process may have been left for the defendant, be stated in the affidavit of the Sheriff or Deputy Sheriff making such service, or otherwise proved by affidavit to the satisfaction of the Judge, before any order is made for perfecting such service.

See Practice in Equity, Rule 102.

SHERIFFS—FEES.

Easter Term, 25 George III, 1785.

124—That the Sheriffs indorse their returns on all Processes delivered to them by the day of their returns respectively, and deliver them to the Attorneys who issued the same. That they attend the Court every Term, by themselves or their under-Sheriffs, and that they appoint Deputies, respectively, who shall always reside in the district in which the Court sits, and as near as convenient to the Court House; who shall always attend the Court in the absence of the High Sheriff; and that all Writs, Rules and Orders delivered to such Deputy, shall be of like effect as if served upon the High Sheriff.

Michaelmas Term, 5 William IV, 1834.

125—In order to secure to Sheriffs the proper emoluments of their office, *It is Ordered*, That, after the first day of Hilary Term next, no costs

---

* The clause bet ween brackets may be omitted in the service of Summary Writs.

7

for the service or return of any Writ or Process, be taxed or allowed in any bill of costs, without the production of such Writ or Process, with the return thereof, signed by the Sheriff or his Deputy, and the fees for the service and return, marked thereupon by such Sheriff or Deputy.

Hilary Term, 4 Victoria, 1841.

126—*Ordered*, That from and after the last day of this term, when any Sheriff, before his going out of office, shall arrest any defendant, and a *Cepi Corpus* shall be returned, he shall and may within the time allowed by Law, be called upon to bring in the body by a rule for that purpose, notwithstanding he may be out of office. before any such rule shall be granted.

SIDE-BAR RULES—RETURN OF WRIT.

Michaelmas Term, 8 Victoria, 1844.

127—*It is Ordered*, That no side-bar rule shall be taken out for the return of any Writ after six months from the day on which such Writ is made returnable ; and that after such six months, motion be made in open Court, or the order of a Judge obtained, before any such rule do issue.

SPECIAL BAIL.

Easter Term, 25 George III, 1785.

128—That there be allowed *twenty* days to all defendants to put in special bail ; and the like number to all plaintiffs to except against such bail, from the time of due notice of bail put in.

Hilary Term, 26 George III, 1786.

129—*Ordered*, That in all process where an affidavit is made and filed of the cause of action, the Sheriffs of the different Counties, at the time of taking the bail bond, shall serve the sureties therein with a copy of such process, subscribed with the following notice :

" A.B."

" Take notice, that unless special bail is put in above by the defendant in this cause within *twenty* days after the return of this process, the condition of the bail bond you have entered into, will be forfeited ?" and upon affidavit made and filed, together with a return of the process by the Sheriff, of the service of such copies as aforesaid, the declaration may be filed *De Bene Esse*, at the return of the process, with notice to plead in *twenty* days ; and if defendant puts in special bail, and doth not plead within time, judgment may be signed ; provided such declaration be filed in the Clerk's Office with notice thereon within *twenty* days after the return of the process.

Michaelmas Term, 59 George III, 1819.

130—*Ordered,* That the time for putting in special bail, agreeably to the rule made in Easter Term, in the twenty-fifth year of His present Majesty's Reign, be enlarged to thirty days.

Michaelmas Term, 6 George IV, 1825.

131—*Ordered,* That if any person or persons, who are, or who hereafter shall become bail in this Court for any defendant, in any action whatever, shall be impleaded by action of debt upon the recognizance in such suit acknowledged, such person or persons shall have liberty to surrender such defendant by the space of twenty entire days next after the return of the Writ of Capias *ad respondendum* or other Process sued out against such bail ; and upon notice thereof, given to the plaintiff of his Attorney, in the suit aforesaid, all further proceedings against such bail upon the recognizance aforesaid, shall cease.

Hilary Term, 2 William IV, 1832.

132—1st. *It is Ordered,* That in all cases, where bail is put in before a Commissioner, the bail-piece, together with the affidavit of the due taken thereof shall be forthwith transmitted, by the Attorney who puts in the bail, to one of the Judges of this Court ; and the notice of bail, in such cases, shall specify the Judge to whom the bail-piece has been so transmitted, as well as the Commissioner, before whom the bail was put in, and the names and additions of the bail.

2nd. That plaintiffs shall be allowed twenty days, after service of the notice of bail, to except against such bail ; and such exception shall be entered with the Judge before whom bail was put in, or to whom the bail-piece has been transmitted, as the case may be.

3rd. That defendants shall be allowed twenty days, after service of notice of exception, to procure their bail to justify, or to add other bail, who shall justify within the said twenty days, unless in either case, upon application made before the said twenty days expire, the the Court, or a Judge, shall see fit to extend the time.

4th. That bail shall justify in open Court, or before the Judge with whom the exception is entered, notice of justifying being first duly given ; and that in all cases, when the bail reside more than ten miles from the place where they are to justify, they may justify by affidavit without personal attendance.

5th. That bail must be Housekeepers or Freeholders; and, in cases where the sum sworn to, does not exceed three hundred pounds, must be worth double the sum sworn to ; and in cases above three hundred pounds, must be worth three hundred pounds more than the sum sworn to, over and above their just debts, and every other sum for which they are bail.

6th. That the affidavit of justification shall be according to the following form ; and may be made before a Judge or a Commissioner of this Court for taking affidavits.

Form of Affidavit.

In the Supreme Court,
Between, etc.

A. B. and C. D., bail for the defendant in this cause, severally make oath and say, and first this deponent, A. B., for himself saith, that he is a Housekeeper, (or Freeholder, as the case may be) residing at (describing particularly the place of residence,) that he is possessed of property to the amount of £ —— (double the amount of the sum sworn to, if under £300, and if above £300, the amount of the sum sworn to, and £300 added thereto) over and above all his just debts, (if bail in any other action add) and every other sum for which he is now bail— (if not bail in any other action, add) that he is not bail for any defendant except in this action; that this deponent's property to the amount of the said sum of £——, (and if bail in any other action, "and of all other sums for which he is now bail as aforesaid") consists of real property of the value of £——, and of personal property of the value of £——, (as the case may be) and this deponent, C. D., for himself saith (as before.)

Sworn, etc.

7th. That if the Notice of bail shall be accompanied by such an affidavit of justification, and the plaintiff afterwards except to such bail, he shall, if such bail are allowed, pay the costs of justification ; and, if such bail are rejected, the defendant shall pay the costs of opposition, unless the Court, or a Judge, shall otherwise order.

8th. That, in cases of exception, when bail have duly justified and been allowed, and a rule for an allowance has been entered, in Court, or an order therefor made by a Judge, and a copy of such rule or order has been served on the plaintiff's Attorney, the bail shall be deemed perfected; and the Attorney who puts in the bail shall forthwith obtain the bail-piece from the Judge, with whom it lies, and file the same with the Clerk.

9th. That if the plaintiff does not except against the bail, within twenty days after service of notice of bail, the bail shall, in like manner, be deemed perfected ; and the Attorney who puts in the bail, shall forthwith, after the expiration of the said twenty days, obtain the bail-piece from the Judge, and file the same with the Clerk.

10th. That, in cases of render in discharge of bail, the Clerk, upon production of the certificate of the Sheriff, to whose custody the defendant has been committed, that such defendant is in his custody, together with an affidavit of the service of notice of render upon the plaintiff's Attorney, shall indorse upon the bail-piece an EXONERETEUR, in the words following : "The bail within named are exonerated ;" and shall set down the day of the month and year of his so doing, and sign his name thereto ; and such certificate and affidavit shall thereupon be filed with the bail-piece.

11th. That hereafter proceedings against bail, in an action upon the recognizance, shall not cease, as provided for in the rule of this Court of Michaelmas Term, one thousand eight hundred and twenty-five, without the costs incurred in such action up to the time of notice of render being first paid.

12th. That any former Rules of this Court, inconsistent with any or these present Rules, relating to bail, shall be hereafter of no effect.

13th. That any Attorney, who shall neglect to transmit, or to file the bail-piece, as the case may be, according to the foregoing Rules, shall be deemed to be in contempt of the Court for disobedience to its rules.

Michaelmas Term, 5 William IV, 1834.

133—*Ordered,* That it shall be deemed irregular to put in bail before a Commissioner, in any parish or City in the Province, in which one or more of the Judges of this Court may reside, unless at times when such Judge or Judges may be absent from their place of residence ; and further, that always, during the sitting of the Court in Term time, it shall be irregular to put in bail before a Commissioner, in the parish of Fredericton, in the County of York ; and that no Judge do receive any bail-piece, transmitted to him, in which the bail may have been entered contrary to this Rule.

SPECIAL CASES.

See Demurrers and Special Cases, No. 45.

SPECIAL CONSENT RULE.

See No. 116.

SPECIAL AND CROWN PAPER.
Hilary Term, 7 George IV, 1826.

134—*Ordered,* That the Clerk of the Crown do keep a paper to be called the Crown paper, in which shall be entered demurrers, and other special matters for argument on the Crown side ; and that the Clerk of the Pleas do in like manner keep a paper, to be called the Special paper, in which shall be entered all demurrers, and other Special matters, for argument on the Plea side : such entries to stand on such papers respectively, in the order in which they may be made, with the said respective Clerks ; and that all the matters contained in the said papers shall come on to be argued on the *Monday in the second week* in each Term, in the order in which they are entered, always beginning with the Crown paper.

Michaelmas Term, 6 William IV, 1835.

135—*It is Ordered,* That the matters contained in the Crown Paper and Special Paper, respectively, shall come on to be argued on the *second day* in each term, any former rule to the contrary notwithstanding.

See Nos, 77, 79, 80.

STUDENTS AND ATTORNEYS EXAMINATION OF—
BY WHOM.

Michaelmas Term, 11 Victoria, 1847.

136—*It is Ordered*, That the Examination of persons desirous of becoming Students, or being admitted as Attorneys of this Court, shall be conducted by the Benchers of the Barristers' Society, as provided for by the said Rules and Regulations; and that no person be entered as a Student, or sworn and enrolled as an Attorney of this Court, or admitted as a Barrister, unless he produce a certificate to be granted pursuant to the said Rules; Provided that this order do not extend to Barristers from other parts of Her Majesty's Dominions, applying to be admitted Barristers here; and provided also, that nothing herein contained shall extend or be construed to impair or interfere with the general superintending power and authority of this Court over all or any of the matters aforesaid.

It is further Ordered, That such of the Rules and Orders of this Court as are inconsistent with the said Rules and Regulations of the Barristers' Society, or so far as they regulate matters therein provided for, (excepting as aforesaid,) be suspended until the further order of the Court in the premises.

See Attorneys, Barristers, etc.

SUBPŒNA

Michaelmas Term, 6 William IV, 1835.

137—*It is Ordered*, That the names of any number of Witnesses may be put in one Writ of Subpœna.

Trinity Term, 12 Victoria, 1849.

Subpœna to prove Execution of Deeds in order to be Registered.

138—*Whereas* by the Act of Assembly 10th Victoria, cap. 42, it is enacted, "That process of Subpœna may be issued out of the Supreme Court of Judicature as in ordinary cases, (and in such form as the said Court may by general rule or order prescribe,) to compel the attendance of any witness, or the production of any conveyance or instrument for the due proof thereof, in order to be registered agreeably to the provisions of this Act; and such Court shall have the like power to punish disobedience to any such Subpœna, in the same manner and to the same extent as in other cases; provided that no such witness shall be compelled to produce; under such Subpœna, any writing or other document that he would not be compelled to produce on a trial:" *It is Ordered*, That the several processes of Subpœna to be used under and in pursuance of the above recited Act, shall be in the form or to the effect following:

NO. I.—SUBPŒNA AD TESTIFICANDUM.

Victoria, by the Grace of God, of the United Kingdom of Great Britain and Ireland, Queen, Defender of the Faith.

To A. B., [*names of the witness or witnesses*] Greeting :—

We command you that, laying aside all and singular business and excuses, you and every of you be and appear in your proper persons before [name and description of the Court, Judge, or other Officer before whom proof is to be-made,] at [the place or office were proof is to be made,] on——the——day of——, at——of the clock in the——noon of the same day, to testify all and singular those things which you or either of you know concerning the execution. of a certain [describe the conveyance or instrument to be proved,] purporting to be made between [the parties to the deed or instrument,] and bearing date the ——day of——, A.D. 18 , to which [deed or instrument] you and each of you were severally a subscribing witness or witnesses ; and further to prove the execution of the said——*, in order that the same may be duly registered according to the provisions of the Act of Assembly in such case made and provided ; and this you or any of you shall in no wise omit, under the penalty upon each of you of one hundred pounds ——Witness——Esquire, at Fredericton,, the——day of——, in the ——year of our Reign.

NO. 2.—SUBPŒNA DUCES TECUM.

[The same as the above to the asterisk*, then thus]—and also that you bring with you, and produce at the time and place aforesaid, the said [describe the deed or instrument] hereinbefore mentioned and described. in order that the same may be duly registered, etc, [conclude as in the preceding form.]

SUMMARY ACTION.

Trinity Term, 5 William IV, 1834.

139—1st. *It is Ordered*, That the Writ in Summary Actions shall be on the Parchment, according to the usage in this Court in other actions.

2nd. That in every action which has not been agreed, and in which it is intended to proceed, the plaintiff's Attorney shall file the Writ, and enter the cause at the term in which the Writ is returnable, and shall make a Docket of such causes, and deliver the same to the Clerk, and pay the fees in like manner as in other actions.

3rd. That in actions to be tried at Nisi Prius, the Writ and Plea shall be delivered from the files of this Court to the plaintiff's Attorney, and shall form the record, and be filed as such, at the Court of Nisi Prius.

4th. That the result of trials at Nisi Prius shall be entered in a brief and summary form, according to the circumstances of each case, and endorsed on the Writ, or annexed thereto, in the nature of a Postea, and returned by the Clerk of the Circuits accordingly.

5th. That the Clerk of this Court shall not, in any case, sign final Judgment, unless the Writ be on file in his office ; and in every Memorandum of Judgment; there shall be reference made to such Writ so on file.

Michaelmas Term, 2 Victoria, 1838.

140—*Ordered*, That in future, in Summary Actions tried at Nisi Prius, a copy of the plea, instead of the original plea, may be filed in the Court of Nisi Prius as a part of the record.

SURVIVING PARTIES.

Trinity Term, 22 Victoria, 1859.

141—In summary causes, when one of the several plaintiffs or defendants shall happen to die after the commencement of the action, the subsequent proceedings shall be in the name of or against the surviving plaintiff or plaintiffs, or defendant or defendants, as the case may be describing him or them respectively, as survivor or survivors of A.B., who bath died since the commencement of this suit, and who was a joint plaintiff or defendant therein.

TAXATION OF COSTS.

See Bill and Taxation.

TRIAL.

See New Trial.

TRIALS AT NISI PRIUS.

Hilary Term, 7 George IV, 1826.

142—In order to prevent inconvenience and delay in the trial of causes at Nisi Prius.

1st. *It is Ordered*, That no record of Nisi Prius shall be received at any Circuit Court in any County in this Province, unless the same shall be delivered, to be entered with the Clerk of the Circuits, at or before the opening of the Court, on the first day of the sittings, unless the Judge, in his discretion, under special circumstances, shall allow the Clerk to receive a Record, and enter the cause for trial after the time above limited; and that every cause shall be tried in the order in which it shall be so entered, beginning with *Remanets*, unless it shall be made out to the satisfaction of the Judge, in open Court, that there is reasonable cause to the contrary, who thereupon may make such order for the trial of the cause so to be put off, as to him shall seem just.

2nd. *Ordered*, That a list of all the causes, entered as aforesaid, shall be made by the Clerk of the Circuits, and by him delivered to the Judge as soon as practicable after the entry so made.

Michaelmas Term, 36 Victoria, 1872.

143—*It is Ordered*, That the Clerks of the Circuits shall not hereafter enter any cause on the Docket at Nisi Prius, unless the Nisi Prius Record is regularly and properly made up, and duly filed with the Clerk at the time of the entry, and that after being so filed, no such Record shall be altered or taken off the files during the Circuit without leave of the Court.

See Rule 89.

ISSUES IN LAW AND IN FACT.

Hilary Term, 43 Victoria, 1880.

144—*It is Ordered*, That no cause in which issues in law and in fact are joined, shall hereafter be entered for trial at any Circuit, until the issues in law are disposed of, unless the plaintiff, when he enters the cause, intends to try it in its order when it is reached on the Docket.

TRIAL BY RECORD.

Trinity Term, 3 Victoria, 1840.

145—*It is Ordered*, That in any case of trial by the Record, it shall be sufficient for the party to make up and deliver to the Chief Justice one paper book, instead of delivering books to all the Judges, unless the Court should otherwise order in any particular case.

Trinity Term, 9 Victoria, 1846.

146—*Ordered*, That in future all cases of trial by the record be entered upon a separate paper, to be called the "Record Trial Docket," which shall be taken up immediately after the motion paper is concluded; the entries to be made in open Court on the first day of each term, and to stand in the docket in the order in which they may be made, unless the Court should otherwise direct ; and that eight days' notice be given of all such trials by the record.

Hilary Term, 13 Victoria, 1850.

147—1st. *It is Ordered*, That if the party, who may have given the notice of trial by the record, pursuant to the Rule of Trinity Term, 9th Victoria, shall not enter the same for trial on the first day of term, as required by such rule, the other party may move to enter the same for trial on the second day of term, and proceed to trial at such time as the Court may thereupon appoint, on delivering to the Chief Justice a paper book, in case such book should not already have been delivered.

2nd. *It is further Ordered*, That either party may give notice of trial by the record, and enter the same pursuant to the Rule of Trinity Term, 9th Victoria—but that if notice be given by both parties, the

8 ·

notice of the party seeking to perfect the record shall have precedence, provided he duly enter the case, and deliver the paper book to the Chief Justice.

Trinity Term, 36 Victoria, 1872.

Venue.

148—No venue shall be changed (unless by consent ot parties) without the special order of the Court, or a Judge, founded upon a Rule Nisi or Summons.

WARRANTS OF ATTORNEY.

See Awards and Warrants.

WARRANT OF ATTORNEY TO CONFESS JUDGMENT.

See No. 31.

WITNESSES—EXAMINATION OF.

See No. 58.

WRITS.

See Records, etc.

WRITS OF ASSISTANCE.

Hilary Term, 59 George III, 1819.

149—*It is Ordered*, That the Writs of assistance to the Officers of His Majesty's Customs in this Province, do issue out of this Court, from time to time, according to the practice of the Exchequer in England.

WRITS OF ATTACHMENT.

Trinity Term, 23 Victoria, 1860.

150—Where Writs of Attachment or other Writs are issued out of the Crown Office upon a Rule of Court therefor, or by order of a Judge, the Clerk shall at the time of signing and sealing the Writ, put at the foot thereof, or indorse thereon, a memorandum in the form following, or to that effect, as the case may be :

"By Rule of Court of ——— Term, A.D. 18—," *or* "By Order of the Chief Justice or Mr. Justice ———, dated ———, filed in the Crown Office.

See No. 15.

WRITS OF ERROR.

Trinity Term, 8 George IV, 1827.

151—*It is Ordered,*—That henceforth no Writ of Error *Coram Nobis* shall be allowed but in open Court ; and then on affidavit of the Error to be assigned.

WRITS OF SCIRE FACIAS.

Hilary Term, 9 George IV, 1828.

152—*It is Ordered*, That from henceforth all defendants in Scire Facias have twenty days to appear from the return day of the Scire Facias; and that, where a defendant appears in Scire Facias, there shall be the like time for pleading as in other actions in this Court.

Hilary Term, 2 Victoria, 1839.

153—*Ordered*, That the Writ of Scire Facias to be issued under the Act of Assembly, 26 George III, c. 24, shall be in the form following, or to that effect; adding in the body of the same any special matter which in particular cases may be deemed requisite.

Victoria, etc. To the Sheriff of Greeting:

Whereas A.B., lately in our Court before us at Fredericton, impleaded C.D. and E.F. in a plea of (the said C.D. having been duly taken and brought into Court by virtue of process issued in the said suit against the said C.D. and E.F. and the said E.F. not having been taken and brought into Court by virtue of such process) and did afterwards by the judgment of the same Court recover as well against the said E.F. as the said C.D. [*state the recovery*] in the same manner as if they had both been taken and brought into Court, pursuant to the Act of Assembly in such case made and provided, whereof the said C.D. and E.F. are convicted as by the record and proceedings thereof still remaining in our same Court manifestly appear.

And now on behalf of the said A.B. in our same Court, we are informed that although judgment be thereupon given, yet satisfaction of the [debt and] damages aforesaid still remains to be made to him: and he is desirous of executing an Execution for such [debt and] damages against the body, or the lands or goods, the sole property of the said E.F., whereof the said A.B. hath humbly besought us to provide him a proper remedy in this behalf; And we being willing that what is just in this behalf should be done, command you that by honest and lawful men of your Bailiwick, you make known to the said E.F., that he be before us at Fredericton, on to show if he has or knows of any thing to say for himself, why the said A.B. ought not to have execution for the [debt and] damages aforesaid, to be executed against the body, or the lands or goods, the sole property of him, the said E.F., according to the force, form and effect of the said recovery, and pursuant to the said Act of Assembly in such case made and provided, if it shall seem expedient for him so to do; and further to do and receive what our said Court before us shall then and there consider of him in his behalf; and have you there the names of those by whom you shall so make known to him, and this Writ.

Witness, etc.

Easter Term, 34 Victoria, 1870.

Return of Moneys Paid.

154—*Ordered.* That the Clerk in Equity do, on the first day of each Term, furnish for the information of the Judges and any parties interested, a detailed return of all moneys in the Bank of New Brunswick, or elsewhere, paid in this Court, or in the Court in Equity, or by direction of either, with the name of the cause, the amount paid in each cause, whether paid in, in every case to the credit of the specific cause, or how otherwise; the date of payment and the amount of increase or interest (if any) in each case, and the amount (if any) drawn out in each cause, with the date or respective dates thereof, and by what authority drawn: a copy of which return shall be entered at length in the Minutes of the Term.

Michaelmas Term, 35 Victoria, 1871.

Moneys—Deposit Place.

155—1st. *It is Ordered,* That hereafter all moneys paid into the Supreme Court, or the Supreme Court in Equity, shall, unless otherwise specially ordered, be paid into the Bank of New Brunswick to the credit of the Supreme Court, or the Supreme Court in Equity and to the credit of the particular cause or matter in which the same shall be paid in: and a deposit receipt thereof shall be forthwith delivered to the Clerk of the Pleas or Clerk in Equity, as the case may be; and no money shall be considered as properly paid in till such deposit receipt is so filed.

2nd. No moneys paid into Court shall be drawn out except by order of the Court, or of a Judge thereof, to be signed by the Clerk and countersigned by the presiding Judge of the Court, or the Judge who make the same; and no such order shall be made unless it be first certified to the Court or Judge, by the Clerk, that such money has been duly deposited and the deposit receipt filed and entered.

3rd. The Clerk of the Pleas and Clerk in Equity shall keep Books in which such receipts shall be entered immediately on the same being filed with him; and such Books shall be open to public inspection at all reasonable times.

GENERAL RULES.

Hilary Term, 1875.

156—The following Rules and Regulations shall hereafter be observed in proceedings in Equity:

NOTICES OF MOTIONS.

That in all cases where no other time is fixed by any Act of Assembly or Rule of this Court, every notice of motion, and every petition, notice of which is necessary, shall be served at least six clear days before the first day of the Sitting of the Court at which such motion or petition is to be heard.

EXCEPTIONS.

Exceptions to a defendant's answer, or to a plaintiff's answer to interrogatories filed by the defendant, may, when submitted to a Judge according to the directions of the Act 17 Victoria, cap. 18, sub-chap. 2, section 10, be set down for argument on the order of the Judge—fourteen days' notice of the time appointed for the argument to be given to the opposite party.

BILLS FOR FORECLOSURE.

In every bill filed for the foreclosure or redemption of a mortgage, the time or times appointed for the payment of the principal money and interest secured by the mortgage, shall be briefly stated.

BILLS OF COSTS.

Every bill of costs presented for taxation shall shew whether the decree or order was made *pro confesso*, upon demurrer, on evidence, or otherwise; and shall also state the respective dates of filing the bill, answer, etc., and of the several motions, hearings, etc., in the cause. No charge shall be allowed for a copy of the bill of costs to file.

GENERAL RULES.

157—The following Rules and Regulations, made pursuant to "The Common Law Procedure Act, 1873," shall be in force :

SEVERAL COUNTS.

1. Except as hereinafter provided, several counts on the same cause of action shall not be allowed, and any count or counts used in violation of this rule may, on application of the defendant, within a reasonable time, be struck out or amended by the Court or a Judge, on such terms as to costs or otherwise, as such Court or Judge may think fit.

SEVERAL PLEAS.

2. Several pleas, replications, or subsequent pleadings, or several avowries or cognizances, founded on the same ground of answer or defence, shall not be allowed : Provided, that on an application to the Court or a Judge to strike out any count, or on an objection taken before a Judge on a summons for leave to plead several matters, to the allowance of several pleas, replications or subsequent pleadings, avowries or cognizances, on the ground of such counts or other pleadings being in violation of this Rule, the Court or Judge may allow such counts on the same cause of action, or such pleas, replications, or subsequent pleadings, or such avowries or cognizances founded on the same ground of answer or defence, as may appear to such Court or Judge to be proper for determining the real question in controversy between the parties on its merits, subject to such terms as to costs and otherwise, as the Court or Judge may think fit.

SERVING DECLARATION.

3. When a defendant appears, a copy of the declaration, with a notice to plead in twenty days, shall be served on his Attorney, or on the defendant if he appears in person ; and on default of his pleading within twenty days after such service, the plaintiff may sign judgment by default,—a plea being first demanded after the said twenty days.

INTERLOCUTORY JUDGMENTS.

4. From and after the present Term, in every memorandum of Interlocutory Judgment, the date of the entry of the cause shall be stated in the margin, or at the foot of the memorandum.

AFFIDAVITS.

5. From and after the first day of April next, every affidavit to be used in any cause or civil proceeding, either on the Common Law or Equity side of the Supreme Court, shall be drawn up in the first person, and shall be divided into paragraphs ; and every paragraph shall be numbered consecutively, and, as nearly as may be, shall be confined to a distinct portion of the subject. No costs shall be allowed for any affidavit, or part of an affidavit, substantially departing from this Rule.

JUDGMENT ROLLS.

6. No entry shall be made on any judgment roll, of any warrants of Attorney to sue or defend.

NISI PRIUS RECORDS.

7. No *placita, jurata*, or award of *venire* shall be entered on the Nisi Prius Record.

All Rules of Court heretofore made, inconsistent with the present Rules, are hereby rescinded.

The following Forms of Proceedings shall be used in the cases to which they are applicable, with such variations as the nature of the action, the character of the parties, or the circumstances of the case may render necessary; but any variance therefrom, not being in matter of substance, shall not affect their validity or regularity.

NO. I.—FORM OF JUDGMENT BY DEFAULT.

IN THE SUPREME COURT.

The   day of   in the year of our Lord one thousand eight hundred and [date of the declaration.]

(Venue.)—A. B. by C. D., his Attorney (or, in person, as the case may be), sued E. F., who had been summoned to answer the said A. B. by virtue of a writ issued on the   day of   in the year of our Lord one thousand eight hundred and   out of Her Majesty's Supreme Court at Fredericton; for etc., [copy the declaration to the end.] And the said E. F. has not appeared; wherefore the said A. B. ought to recover against him on occasion of the premises.* And the said A. B. prays that the amount to be recovered in this action may be ascertained and assessed by the Court; and thereupon it is proved, and appears to the Court that the said A. B. ought to recover against the said E. F. the sum of   Therefore it is considered that the said A. B. do recover against the said E. F. the said sum of   so ascertained and assessed by the Court, and also   for his costs of suit by the Court here adjudged to the said A. B., which, in the whole amount to.

If the damages have been assessed on a Writ of Inquiry, proceed as follows, after the asterisk in the above Form:

But because it is unknown to the Court what damages the said A. B. has sustained by means of the premises, the Sheriff of the said County of   is commanded that by the oaths of seven good and lawful men of his Bailiwick he inquire thereof, and that he send the inquisition which he shall thereupon take, to our Supreme Court at Fredericton, on etc., [the return day of the writ of inquiry,] under his seal, and the seals of the said jurors. At which day, before our said Court comes the said A. B. by his said Attorney, and the said Sheriff returns the inquisition taken before him in the said County, on the   day of   in the year, etc., by which it is found that the said A. B. has sustained damages by means of the premises, to the sum of   . Therefore it is considered that the said A. B. do recover against the said E. F. the said sum of   so found by the said inquisition, and also   for his costs," etc., [as above.]

If the judgment is on confession, proceed as follows after the declaration :
And the said E. F. in person, (or, by   his Attorney, as the case may
be) comes and says that he cannot deny the action of the said A. B. in the
declaration mentioned, and acknowledges that the said A. B. is entitled to
recover against him the said E. F. the sum of   . Therefore it is considered that the said A. B. do recover against the said E. F. the sum of
        so acknowledged ; and also   for his costs, etc., [as above.]

NO. 2.—FORM OF JUDGMENT OF NON PROS.

IN THE SUPREME COURT.

The   day of   in the year of our Lord one thousand eight
hundred and [date of signing judgment.]

(Venue).—C. D. was served with a copy of a writ of summons, (or,
arrested by virtue of a writ of capias, as the case may be,) issued out of our
Supreme Court at Fredericton, on the   day of   * 'in the year of
our Lord, etc., in an action at the suit of A. B. [if the defendant was
arrested, state : "directed to the Sheriff of the County of '   ,"] and
the said C. D. appeared to the said writ by E. F., his Attorney, (or, in person, as the case may be,) according to the provisions of "The Common
Law Procedure Act, 1873." And the said A. B. hath not declared against
the said C. D., in the said action within the time prescribed by the said Act.
Therefore it is considered that the said A. B. take nothing by his said writ.
And it is further considered by the said Court that the said C. D. do recover
against the said A. B. the sum of   for his costs in this behalf, by the
said Court now adjudged to the said C. D., and that the said C. D. have
execution thereof. etc.

NO. 3.—FORM OF A NISI PRIUS RECORD.

IN THE SUPREME COURT.

The   day of   in the year of our Lord one thousand eight
hundred and [date of the declaration.]

(Venue.)—A. B. by C. D., his Attorney (or, in person, as the case may
be, and as in the declaration), sues E. F., who has been summoned to
answer the said A. B. by virtue of a writ issued on the   day of
in the year of our Lord (the date of the first writ), out of Her Majesty's
Supreme Court of Judicature ; for etc., (copy the declaration to the end,
and all the pleadings, with the dates, writing each plea or pleading in a
separate paragraph, and numbering the same as in the pleading delivered,
and conclude thus): Therefore let a jury come before the Honorable
Her Majesty's Chief Justice, assigned to hold Pleas in the Court of our
Lady the Queen, at Fredericton, on the   day of   , in the
year of our Lord 18 (the first day of the Nisi Prius Sittings), to try the
matters in question between the said parties. (It the cause is to be tried
at a Circuit Court, instead of the above, state as follows: "before the
Honorable   one of the Justices of our Lady the Queen, assigned to
hold the Circuit Court and take the assizes in and for the said County of
on," etc., (the first day of the Circuit Court.)

No. 4.—FORM OF POSTEA ON A VERDICT FOR PLAINTIFF.

Afterwards, on the   day of   A.D. [the first day of the
Sittings, or the Court, as the case may be], at   in the County
of   before the Honorable   Chief Justice,) or, "one of the
Justices of the Supreme Court," as the case may be), come the parties
within mentioned, by their respective Attorneys within mentioned, and
a jury of the said County being summoned, also come, who being sworn
to try the matters in question between the said parties,* upon their
oath say, that [state the affirmative or negative of the issue as it is found
for the plaintiff, and in the terms adopted in this pleading. If there be
several issues joined and tried, say, "as to the first issue within joined
upon their oath say, that " [state the affirmative or negative of the issue
as found for the plaintiff]. "and as to the second issue within joined
the jurors aforesaid upon their oath say that " [proceed to state the
finding of the jury upon all the issues; and conclude with the assessment
of damages thus]: And they assess the damages of the said A.B. on
occasion of the premises within complained of by him, over and above his
costs of suit, at   therefore, etc.

(*Where the verdict is for the defendant, the Postea must be varied to suit
the circumstances*).

NO. 5.—FORM OF POSTEA ON A VERDICT FINDING A BALANCE IN FAVOR
OF A DEFENDANT UNDER A PLEA OF SET-OFF, SECT. 72.

(Proceed as in form No. 4, to the asterisk, then thus): upon their
oath say, (if the first plea was "never indebted," say—that the said
E.F. never was indebted, as within alleged). And as to the second
issue within joined, the jurors aforesaid say, that the said A.B. was
and is indebted to the said E.F., as within alleged, in amount greater than ·
the said A.B's claim in the declaration mentioned, and they find and
assess the balance due from the said A.B., to the said E.F. in respect
thereof, at the sum of   Therefore, etc.

NO. 6.—FORM OF JUDGMENT FOR PLAINTIFF ON A VERDICT.

[*Copy the Nisi Prius Record to the end of the Postea, and then proceed
thus*]: Afterwards, on the   day of   in the year of our Lord
(day of signing final judgment), come the parties aforesaid, by their respective Attorneys aforesaid, and the Honorable   Her Majesty's Chief
Justice assigned to hold Pleas in Her Majesty's Supreme Court at Fredericton, (or, "the Honorable   one of the Justices of the Supreme Court
of our Lady the Queen, assigned to hold the Circuit Court and take the
assizes in and for the said County of," etc., as the case may be), before
whom the said issue was (or, "issues were,") tried, hath sent hither his
record, had before him, in these words: Afterwards, etc., (copy the postea).
Therefore it is considered that the said A. B. do recover against the said
E. F. the said moneys by the jurors aforesaid, in form aforesaid assessed,
(or, if the action be in debt, and the jury do not assess the debt, but only
damages for the detention, say "do recover against the defendant the said
debt of   and the damages by the jurors aforesaid assessed) ;" and also

9

for his costs of suit by the Court here adjudged of increase to the said A. B.; which moneys and costs, (or, "debt, damages and costs)," in the whole amount to

NO. 7.—FORM OF JUDGMENT FOR DEFENDANT ON A VERDICT.

[*Proceed as in the preceding Form to the end of the postea then thus*] *:* Therefore it is considered that the said A. B. take nothing by his said writ, and that the said E. F. do go thereof without day, etc.   And it is further considered that the said E. F. do recover against the said A. B.   'for his costs and charges by him about his defence in this behalf expended, by the Court here adjudged to the said E. F., and that the said E. F. have ˉ execution thereof, etc.

NO. 8.—FORM OF JUDGMENT FOR DEFENDANT ON A PLEA OF SET-OFF.

[*Proceed as in the above Form to the end of the postea,. then thus :*] Therefore it is considered that the said A. B. take nothing by his said writ, but that the said E. F. do recover against him the sum of   in form aforesaid found to be due from the said A. B. to the said E. F., together with   for his costs of defence by the Court here adjudged to the said E. F., amounting in the whole to   , and that the said E. F. have execution therefor.

NO. 9.—FORM OF POSTEA ON A VERDICT FOR DEFENDANT IN REPLEVIN, ON A PLEA OF NON CAPIT, UNDER 1 REV. STAT., C. 126, § 15.

Afterwards, etc., *(as in the preceding Form to the asterisk, then thus:)* that the said defendant did take and detain the goods and chattels mentioned in the declaration, as a distress for rent due for certain premises held by the plaintiff under a demise at a certain rent; and that there was due to the defendant for such rent at the time of the distress, and still is due, the sum of   , and they assess the damages of the defendant for the said rent, and the costs and charges of making the distress, at the sum of   , besides his costs of suit, etc.

[*If the bailiff of the landlord, or any one acting in aid of the landlord, be made a defendant, the postea may be varied, as follows :*]   "And that there was due to the defendant C. D. (the landlord) for such rent, etc., (as above) and that the defendant E. F. was at the time of making the said distress, the bailiff of the said C. D. (or, "that the said E. F. was present aiding and assisting the said C. D. in making the said distress)," etc.

NO. 10.—FORM OF JUDGMENT FOR DEFENDANT IN REPLEVIN, UNDER 1 REV. STATUTES, C. 126, § 15.

(Proceed in the usual form to the end of the Postea—then thus:) Therefore it is considered that the said A. B. take nothing by his said writ, and that the said E. F. do go thereof without day, etc.   And it is further considered that the said E. F. do recover against the said A. B. the said sum of   by the jurors aforesaid assessed, and also   for his costs and charges by him about his defence in this behalf expended by the Court here adjudged to the said E. F., which said damages and costs in the whole amount to   and that the said E. F. have execution thereof, etc.

NO. 11.—WRIT OF FIERI FACIAS ON A JUDGMENT FOR PLAINTIFF.

VICTORIA, by the Grace of God, etc.   To the Sheriff of   greeting :
We command you, that of the goods and chattels of C. D. in your
Bailiwick, you cause to be levied and made   * (the amount for
which the judgment is signed), which A. B. lately in our Supreme Court
recovered against him, whereof the said C. D. is convicted as appears by
the record ; and have that money before us at Fredericton, on, etc., [a
return day in Term], to be rendered to the said A. B.   And in what
manner you shall have executed this our writ, make appear to us at the
return hereof; and have you there then this writ. Witness, etc., [the
date of issuing].

NO. 12.—WRIT OF FIERI FACIAS ON A JUDGMENT FOR DEFENDANT.

VICTORIA, by the Grace of God, etc., (as in the preceding form, to the
asterisk), which lately in our Supreme Court were awarded to C. D. for the
costs of defence in an action lately prosecuted in our said Court by the said
A. B. against the said C. D., whereof the said A. B. is convicted : (If a verdict has been given in favor of the defendant for a balance, on a plea of set-
off, state thus) : "were awarded to C. D. according to the provisions of
'The Common Law Procedure Act, 1873,' as well for a balance found due
to him from the said A. B. in an action lately prosecuted in our said Court
by the said A. B. against the said C. D., as for the costs of defence of the
said action ; whereof the said A. B. is convicted ") : and have that money
before us, etc., (as in the preceding Form.)

NO. 13.—WRIT OF FIERI FACIAS ON A JUDGMENT FOR DEFENDANT IN
REPLEVIN.

VICTORIA, by the Grace of God, etc., (as in Form No. 11 to the asterisk)
which lately in our Supreme Court were awarded to the said C. D. in an
action of replevin lately prosecuted against him by the said A. B. in our
said Court,* as well for unlawfully taking the goods and chattels of the said
C. D. as for the costs of defence of the said action ; whereof the said A. B.
is convicted : and have that money before us, etc., (conclude as in Form
No. 12.)

If the goods have not been restored to the defendant, and the value of
them is awarded in damages under 1 Rev. Stat., cap. 126, proceed as above
to the asterisk—then thus): as well for the value of certain goods and
chattels of the said C. D. unlawfully taken by the said A. B., and for the
said unlawful taking, as for the costs of defence of this said action, whereof,
etc.

(If the goods replevied have been taken as a distress for rent, the form
of the execution may be varied to suit the circumstances).

GENERAL RULES

OF

THE ELECTION COURT.

General Rules made under and by virtue of the Act of the Dominion of Canada passed in the 37th year of Her Majesty's Reign, Chapter 10, being "*The Dominion Controverted Elections Act, 1874.*"

158—1. An Election Petition shall contain the following statements :—

(a) The right of the Petitioner to petition within Section seven of the Act ;

(b) The holding and result of the Election ;

(c) A brief statement of the facts and grounds relied on to sustain the prayer :

And shall conclude with a prayer for such relief as the Petitioner claims to be entitled to.

2. The Petition shall be divided into paragraphs to be numbered consecutively, each of which, as nearly as may be, shall be confined to a distinct portion of the subject : and no costs shall be allowed for drawing or copying any Petition not substantially in compliance with this Rule, unless otherwise ordered by the Court, or one of the Election Judges.

3. The following form of Petition, or to the like effect, shall be sufficient :—

IN THE ELECTION COURT.

The Dominion Controverted Elections Act, 1874.

Election of a Member from the House of Commons for [*state the County or district*] in the Province of New Brunswick.

The Petition of A. of   (*or*, of A. of   and B. of   , as *the case may be*,) whose name is subscribed (*or*, whose names are subscribed) :

(a) Your Petitioner is a person (*or*, your petitioners are persons) who had a right to vote at the above mentioned Election, (*or*, was a Candidate at the said Election, *as the case may be*.)

(b) That the said Election was held on the   day of A.D. 18   , when A. B. and C. D. were Candidates, and the returning Officer has returned the said A. B. as being duly elected, (*or as the case may be*.)

(c) Your Petitioner says that [*here state the facts and grounds relied on.*] Wherefore your Petitioner prays that it may be determined that the said A. B. was not duly elected and returned, and that the said Election was void, (*or*, that the said C. D. was duly elected, and ought to have been returned; *or as the case may be*.)

Dated the   day of   , A.D. 18

[*Signature.*]

4. Evidence need not be stated in the Petition ; but the Court, or one of the Judges, may order such particulars to be given as may be necessary to prevent surprise and unnecessary expense, and to ensure a fair and effectual trial, in the same manner as in proceedings in the Supreme Court, and upon such terms as to costs, or otherwise, as may be ordered.

5. The Petitioner shall, with the Petition, leave a copy thereof with the Clerk of the Court, to be sent to the returning Officer, pursuant to section eight of the Act.

6. The Petitioner shall leave with the Petition at the Office of the Clerk of the Court, a writing signed by him, or on his behalf, stating the name of some person entitled to practice as an Attorney, whom he authorizes to act as his Agent ; or, stating that he acts for himself, as the case may be ; and in either case, giving an address at which notices addressed to him may be left ; and if no such writing be left, or address given, then notice of objection to the Petition, and all other notices, may be given by posting up the same in the Office of the Clerk of the Court.

7. Any person returned as a Member may at any time after he is returned, file in the Office of the Clerk of the Court, a writing signed by him or on his behalf, appointing a person entitled to practice as an Attorney to act as his Agent in case there should be a Petition against him, or stating that he intends to act for himself ; and in either case, giving an address at which notices in the matter of the Petition may be left : and in default of such writing being filed within a week after service of the Petition, notices may be given and served by posting up the same in the Office of the Clerk of the Court.

8. When a Petitioner claims the seat for an unsuccessful Candidate, alleging that he had a majority of lawful votes, the party complaining of, and the party defending the Election and return, shall each, seven days before the day appointed for trial, deliver to the Clerk of the Court, and also at the address, if any, given by the Petitioner and Respondent (as the case may be), a list of the voters intended to be objected to, and of the heads of objection to each such vote: and the Clerk of the Court shall allow inspection and office copies of such lists to all parties concerned ; and no evidence shall be given against the validity of any vote, nor upon any head of objection not specified in the list, except by leave of the Court, or one of the Judges, upon such terms as to amendment of the list, postponement of the enquiry, and payment of costs, or otherwise, as may be ordered.

9. When, in a Petition complaining of an undue return, and claiming the seat for some person, the Respondent intends to give evidence to prove that the Election of such person was undue, pursuant to the 66th Section of the Act, he shall seven days before the day appointed for trial, deliver to the Clerk of the Court, and also at the address, if any, given by the Petitioner, a list of the objections on which he intends to rely, and the Clerk of the Court shall allow inspection and office copies of such list to all parties concerned ; and no evidence shall be given by a Respondent of any objection to the Election not specified in such list, except by leave of the Court or one of the Judges, upon such terms as to amendment of the list, postponement of the inquiry, and payment of costs, as may be ordered.

10. The Clerk of the Court shall keep a Book or Books in which he shall record all the proceedings of the Court ; the date of filing each Petition ; notice of preliminary objections ; withdrawal or substitution ; and the decision in each case tried;—the proceedings in each case to be kept

separately. He shall also keep a record of the names and addresses of the agents given by either of the parties; which books shall be open to inspection by any person during office hours, without payment of any fee.

11. When it shall be made to appear to a Judge by affidavit, within five days after the presentation of a petition, that there is reasonable ground to believe that such petition cannot be served upon the respondent within the time limited by the ninth section of the Act, such Judge may allow further time for effecting such service. And in case service cannot be effected within the time so appointed, and the respondent has named an agent, or given an address, then the service may be made upon such agent personally, or by posting the copy in a registered letter to the address given, within such time as the Judge may, on proof of the fact by affidavit, direct.

12. If no agent has been appointed, or address given by the respondent, and it is made to appear by affidavit to the satisfaction of a Judge, that service of the petition cannot be made upon the respondent personally, or at his domicile, such Judge may order that a notice of the presentation of the petition and the prayer thereof, shall be affixed in a conspicuous place in the Office of the Clerk of the Court ; and such notice shall be deemed equivalent to personal service of the petition.

13. Preliminary objections to a petition, under the tenth section of the Act, shall be filed in the Office of the Clerk of the Court; and notice thereof, and that a copy has been filed for the petitioner; shall be forthwith served by the respondent upon the petitioner or his agent.

14. Either party may apply for an order fixing the time and place for hearing the preliminary objections.

15. The answer of the respondent shall be filed with the Clerk of the Court. It shall be divided into paragraphs, numbered consecutively; and each paragraph shall be confined, as near as may be, to a distinct portion of the subject. Notice of the filing the answer shall be forthwith served by the respondent on the petitioner, or his agent.

16. The application to fix a time and place for the trial of a petition, shall be made in writing to the Judge assigned for the trial of election petitions in the County to which such petition relates; and the application shall state the time when such petition was filed, and when it was at issue.

17. The Judge's Order fixing the time and place of trial, shall be delivered to the Clerk of the Court, who shall post up the same in a conspicuous place in his Office, and shall send a notice thereof by post to the Sheriff of the County to which it relates, so that he may receive the same at least fourteen days before the day appointed for trial; and such Sheriff shall forthwith publish the same in the said County. The cost of publication of this and any other matter required to be published by the Sheriff, shall be paid by the petitioner, or the person at whose instance the same is published, and, shall form part of the general costs of the petition.

18. The notice of trial may be in the following form :

IN THE ELECTION COURT.

The Dominion Controverted Elections Act, 1874.

Election Petition for the County of

Between A. B, [*name of petitioner*] Petitioner, and C. D. Respondent.

Take notice that the above petition will be tried at   on the
day of   , and on such subsequent days as may be needful.

Dated the   day of   , 18

By Order of Mr. Justice ———.

W. C., Clerk of the Court.

19. A copy of such notice shall be served upon the respondent, or his agent, or upon the petitioner, or his agent, (as the case may be) by the party who obtains the order, at least fourteen days before the day appointed for the trial. ,

20. Notice of the time and place of the trial of each election petition shall be sent by post by the Clerk of the Court to the Secretary-Treasurer of the County for which the election complained of shall have been held, or to such officer as may have the custody of the poll books and check lists used at the said election; and the said Secretary-Treasurer or other officer shall forthwith deliver to the Registrar of the Judge who is to try the petition, or his Deputy, the said poll books and check lists, for which the Registrar or his Deputy shall give, if required, a receipt; and the Registrar or his Deputy shall keep the said poll books and check lists in safe custody until the conclusion of the trial, and then return the same to the said Secretary-Treasurer or other officer.

21. The Judge assigned to try the petition, or, in case of his absence or inability, any other Judge of the Court may by order postpone the commencement of the trial till such day as he may appoint ; and notice thereof shall be forthwith sent by the Clerk of the Court to the Sheriff of the County in which the trial is to take place, and the said Sheriff shall publish the same. Notice thereof shall also be forthwith served by the party obtaining the same, upon the opposite party.

22. In the event of the Judge not having arrived at the time appointed for the trial, or to which the trial is postponed, the commencement of the trial, shall, *ipso facto,* stand adjourned to the ensuing day, and so from day to day until the arrival of the Judge.

23. No formal adjournment of the Court for the trial of an election petition shall be necessary ; but the trial is to be deemed adjourned, and may be continued from day to day until the enquiry is concluded ; and in the event of the Judge who begins the trial, being disabled by illness or otherwise, it may be recommenced and concluded by any other of the Judges.

24. All affidavits, notices, and other papers in any matter in the Court for the trial of an election petition, may be entitled as follows:

IN THE ELECTION COURT.

The Dominion Controverted Elections Act, 1874.

Election Petition for the County of

Between A. B., [*name of petitioner*] Petitioner, and C. D., Respondent.

25. The Judge assigned to try an election petition shall appoint an officer to attend at the trial, who shall be called the Registrar of the Court, and who shall, in person or by Deputy, perform all the functions incident to the Officer of a Court of Record, and such other duties as may be prescribed to him. He shall keep a book in which shall be entered the proceedings of each trial, as in a trial at Circuit; and at the conclusion of the trial shall send such book, together with any papers or documents filed with him during the trial, to the Clerk of the Election Court.

26. At the time appointed for the trial of any election petition, the petitioner shall leave with the Registrar, for the use of the Judge, a legibly written, or printed copy of the petition, and of all the proceedings necessary to show the matters to be tried—including the particulars of objection on either side; the correctness of which, so far as the proceedings are filed with the Clerk of the Court, shall be certified by him. The Judge may allow amendment of the said copy. In default of such copy being delivered, the Judge may refuse to try the petition, or may allow further time for delivery of the copy, or may adjourn the trial, in every case, upon such terms as to costs and otherwise, as he shall see fit.

27. A Judge's order to compel the attendance of a witness may be in the following form :

IN THE ELECTION COURT FOR THE COUNTY OF ——

To C. D. [*name and residence*]: You are hereby required to attend before the said Court at [*place*] on   the   day of   at the hour of   (or, forthwith, as the case may be), to be examined as a witness in the matter of an Election Petition between E. F., Petitioner, and G. H., Respondent, and to attend the said Court till your examination shall be completed.

Dated the   day of   A. B., *Judge of said Court.*

28. A warrant of commitment for contempt may be as follows :

To the Sheriff of the County of   , and to any Constable thereof, and to the Keeper of the Gaol of the said County :

At a Court held at   on the   day of   for the trial of an Election Petition for the County of   before the Honorable one of the Election Judges, pursuant to "The Dominion Controverted Elections Act, 1874 :"

Whereas C. D. was this day adjudged to be guilty of a contempt of the said Court, and was thereupon for his said contempt sentenced to be imprisoned in the County gaol at   , for   days, and to pay a fine of $, and further to be imprisoned in the said gaol till the said fine was paid; these are therefore to command you the said Sheriff, and all Constables and Peace Officers, to take the said C. D. into custody, and convey him to the said gaol, and deliver him into the custody of the Keeper thereof; and the said Keeper is hereby required to receive the said C. D. into his custody and detain him in the said gaol for the times above specified, in pursuance of the said sentence.

Given under my hand and seal this   day of   , A. D. 18·

                A. B.,   [L. S.]   *Judge of the said Court.*

29. Such warrant may be directed to the Sheriff and Peace Officers of any County or place where the person adjudged guilty of contempt may be found ; and may be executed by any or either of the persons to whom it is directed ; and it shall be sufficient authority to the said Sheriff or other Peace Officers, and to the Gaoler, without further particularity.

30. All interlocutory questions and matters may be heard and disposed of before any Judge of the Court, who shall have the same control over the proceedings under the Act as a Judge at Chambers in the ordinary proceedings of the Supreme Court.

31. Notice of an application for leave to withdraw a Petition shall be in writing, signed by the Petitioner or his agent, and shall be left at the Office of the Clerk of the Court. It shall state the grounds on which the application is intended to be supported, and may be in the following form :

IN THE ELECTION COURT, COUNTY OF ———.

The Dominion Controverted Elections Act, 1874.

The Petition of   [*names of Petitioners*] presented this   day of

The Petitioner proposes to withdraw his Petition, upon the following grounds, (state the grounds), and prays that a day may be appointed for hearing his application.

Dated the   day of

[*Signature.*]

32. On filing such application, a Judge may appoint a time and place for the hearing thereof.

33. A copy of the notice of intention to apply to withdraw the Petition shall be served by the Petitioner upon the Respondent or his agent, and also upon the Sheriff of the County, who shall publish the same in the County to which it relates.

34. The said notice may be in the following form :

IN THE ELECTION COURT, COUNTY OF ———.

The Dominion Controverted Elections Act, 1874.

In the Election Petition between   Petitioner and   Respondent.

Notice is hereby given that the above Petitioner did on the   day of   lodge at the Office of the Clerk of the Election Court, notice of an application to withdraw his Petition, on the following grounds, (state the grounds, as in the application). Also, take notice, that the said application will be heard before Mr. Justice   at   on the   day of

Dated, etc.

[*Petitioner's signature.*]

35. Notice of the abatement of a Petition, under the fifty-sixth section of the Act, shall be given by the personal representative of the Petitioner, or by some person interested, by serving a copy thereof on the Respondent, or his agent, and also upon the Sheriff of the County, who shall publish the

10

same in the County to which it relates in the manner hereinafter prescribed.
Such notice may be in the following form :

IN THE ELECTION COURT, COUNTY OF ———.

The Dominion Controverted Elections Act, 1874.

In the Election Petition between   Petitioner and   Respondent.
Notice is hereby given, that the above named Petitioner, (or, the above
named   , the surviving Petitioner, as the case may be), died on the
      day of   , and that the said Petition is thereby abated, according to the fifty-sixth section of the said Act.
Dated the   day of   , A.D.

[Signature.]

36. Within one calendar month after the publication of such notice, any
person intending to apply to be substituted as a Petitioner, may make a
written application for that purpose ; and the Judge to whom such application
is made, shall appoint a time and place for hearing the same, of which
notice shall be given in the manner directed in case of an application to
withdraw a petition. (Rule 33.)

37. If the Respondent dies ; or is summoned to Parliament as a Member
of the Senate ; or if the House of Commons has resolved that his seat is
vacant ; any person entitled to be a Petitioner under the Act in respect of
the election to which the Petition relates, may give notice of the fact in the
County, by causing such notice, (stating with reasonable particularity his
right to be substituted), and signed by him, to be published in at least one
newspaper published therein, if any, and by leaving a copy of such notice
with the Sheriff of the County, and a like copy with the Clerk of the Court.

38. The manner and time of the Respondent giving notice to the Election
Court that he does not intend to oppose the petition, shall be by
delivering a written notice thereof signed by him, at the Office of the Clerk
of the Court, seven days before the day appointed for trial, exclusive of the
day of leaving such notice.

39. Upon such notice being left at the Office of the Clerk of the Court,
he shall forthwith notify the Judge assigned to try the petition, and also send
a copy thereof by post, to the petitioner or his agent, and to the Sheriff of
the County ; and the said Sheriff shall cause the same to be published in
the County in the manner hereinafter directed.

40. The time for applying to be admitted as a Respondent in either of
the events mentioned in the fifty-seventh section of the Act, shall be within
ten days after the publication of the notices thereof respectively, as hereinbefore
directed ; or within such further time as the Court or one of the
Judges may allow.

41. When a Petition is withdrawn under the provisions of the fifty-ninth
section of the Act, notice in writing of such withdrawal, signed by the
Petitioner, addressed to the Clerk of the Election Court, shall be filed in
the Office of the said Clerk. The notice shall be entitled in the cause, and
shall briefly state the facts which authorize the withdrawal of the Petition.

42. Costs shall be taxed by the Clerk of the Court, or by his Deputy specially appointed, upon the Rule of Court or Judge's Order by which the costs are payable; and costs when taxed may be recovered by attachment or execution issued upon the Rule of Court ordering them to be paid. If payable by order of a Judge, then by making such order a Rule of Court in the ordinary way, and issuing an attachment or execution upon such rule against the person by whom the costs are ordered to be paid, or against his goods and chattels; or, in case there be money in Court available for the purpose, then to the extent of such money, by order of the Election Court, or one of the Election Judges. The office fees payable for inspection, office copies, enrolment, and other proceedings under the Act and these Rules, shall be the same as those payable for like proceedings in the Supreme Court.

43. Writs of Subpœna *ad testificandum* and *duces tecum*, under the Seal of the Election Court, may be issued at any time by the Clerk of the Court; which Writs may be in the following form :—

IN THE ELECTION COURT.

Dominion of Canada. } Victoria, by the Grace of
Province of New Brunswick. } God, etc.
To-wit : }

To ————

We command you that, all excuses being laid aside, you and every of you be and appear before our Election Judge, assigned to try the Election Petition for [*name the County*], at , in the County of . on the day of 18 , by o'clock in the noon, and so from day to day until the said Election Petition shall be tried, or otherwise disposed of ; to testify what you (*or*, either of you) know in the matter of the said Petition, wherein is (*or*, are) Petitioner, and is (*or*, are), Respondent, on the part of the , and at the Court for the trial of the said Election Petition for [*name the County*], at aforesaid, to be tried. [*In case of a subpœna duces tecum, add :*]—And also, that you bring with you and produce at the time and place aforesaid [*describing what is to be produced in the ordinary way*].

[*If the subpœna is to attend before the Election Court :*]— Before our said Election Court for the Province of New Brunswick, at Frederict in, on the day of 18 , by o'clock in the noon, to testify all and singular those things which you, or either of you, know in the matter of an Election Petition depending in our said Court at Fredericton [*describing the Petition as above, or other the matter in which the witness is called, as the case may be*]; and also that you bring with you and produce at the time and place aforesaid [*describing what is to be produced as aforesaid*], and this you, or any of you, shall by no means omit, under the penalty upon each of you of one hundred pounds.

Witness the Honorable [*the senior Election Judge*], one of the Judges of our Election Court at Fredericton, the day of 18

(Signed) A. B.,
Clerk of the Election Court.

44. The Clerk of the Pleas in the Supreme Court shall be the Clerk of the Election Court.

45. After the trial of an Election Petition the Judge shall deliver to the Clerk of the Election Court, the evidence and proceedings before the said Judge, and his finding on the said Petition, which shall be filed of record by the said Clerk.

46. Publication of any Petition, paper or notice by the Sheriff, shall, when it is not otherwise expressed in the Act, be by posting printed copies of such Petition, paper or notice on the Court House, in the Offices of the Secretary-Treasurer; and of the Registrar of Deeds for the County to which the Petition relates, and by publishing the same once in a newspaper published in such County, if any. In the City of St. John, the notices shall be posted in the Common Clerk's Office.

47. The word "County," wherever it is used in these Rules, shall also mean "City and County," or "Electoral District," if necessary to give effect to the provisions thereof.

48. No proceedings under "The Dominion Controverted Elections Act, 1874," or under these Rules, shall be defeated by any formal objection.

49. Any Rule made, or to be made in pursuance of the Act, shall be published by a copy thereof being put up in the Office of the Clerk of the Election Court.

> JOHN C. ALLEN, *Chief Justice.*
> J. W. WELDON,
> CHARLES FISHER,
> A. R. WETMORE.
> CHARLES DUFF.

Fredericton, 2nd November, 1878,